THE WAY OF
THE WOODSHOP

THE WAY OF
THE WOODSHOP

CREATING, DESIGNING
& DECORATING WITH WOOD

ALEKSANDRA ZEE

DEY ST.
An Imprint of WILLIAM MORROW

THIS BOOK IS DEDICATED TO YOU, THE READER.
MAY IT IGNITE YOUR CREATIVITY AND INSPIRE YOU TO
FIND BEAUTY IN THE EBB AND FLOW. I MAY NOT KNOW
YOU, OR MAYBE I DO; THESE PAGES ARE FOR YOU.

CONTENTS

THE WAY OF
THE WOODSHOP

INTRODUCTION

I have always loved working with my hands. Whenever I am about to start a new project, I experience a mouthwatering, almost tangible craving. It's been this way since I was a child, whether gathering materials for forts or drawing elaborate chalk murals on my driveway. When I am working with my hands, it's like the world slows down and I become fully present. Everything stops, the autopilot of creativity kicks in, and a flow begins. To me, making is an act of self-care, because it forces me to take a break from the fast-paced world and to return to myself.

As that little girl drawing chalk murals, I never imagined that I would one day be making a living with my hands as a woodworker.

As an art student in college, I dreamed of following in the footsteps of greats like Matisse and Picasso and creating art that was completely unique and original. I wasn't much of a painter, but I tried. And through my experimentation I learned that creative failure is an important part of the artistic journey.

Everything changed when I discovered visual installation art. In a nutshell, installation is a three-dimensional art form that transforms the way we see a space. I fell in love with installation art, spending my spare time dumpster diving for materials for my next project. After college, armed with a degree in fine arts, I interviewed for a junior creative position at Anthropologie, and I got the job. As a visual display coordinator, I would be working on window displays and in-store installations. I packed my bags and moved from my small oceanfront hometown of Dana Point, California, to the Bay Area to work for Anthro.

The job at Anthropologie was like boot camp. We built everything from scratch for those installations, in a studio with every imaginable material at our fingertips. The job was sink or swim: After a brief training session where I was taught the basics—how to properly execute projects and how to use tools safely—I was on my own. Don't know how to sew? No biggie. I was a quick learner. That was my attitude, and I applied it to all sorts of new skills: knotting macramé, dyeing fabric, building tables and headboards, or whatever else was needed. Working with wood quickly became my absolute favorite part of the job. This was also when I met my friend and mentor, Katie Gong, a third-generation woodworker from a family of carpenters, who took me under her wing. As her apprentice, I soaked up her wood wisdom like a sponge. When I was at the wood bench with Katie, I felt like I was home. I had found my calling.

Ten years later, and after several daring leaps (and restaurant jobs to supplement my income), I can officially call myself a working artist. It's not always as glamorous as it may seem. Beyond the inspiration process and the labor of fabricating and putting together pieces, there is a lot of grunt work behind the scenes. Emails, planning, conference calls, supply shopping. While I'd love to be in the studio every day creating, there are a lot of other important parts of running a business, which may be less fulfilling. But one of the big perks of my job is that I get to make my own schedule and every day is different. And it's all mine. A living, breathing business that emerged straight from my heart.

This book will introduce you to the art of working with your hands, and it will show you how to create some gorgeous projects with wood. It's a field guide filled with projects for all skill levels, from absolute beginner to advanced. My intention is to help you gradually build your woodworker's knowledge and confidence, from sourcing lumber, to learning the basics of power tools, to decorating your home. I often teach workshops out of my shop in Oakland, California, and this is a part of my job that I deeply love. In fact, it's the reason that I wrote this book. There is nothing more meaningful to me than sharing the knowledge that I have gained over the years with my students and watching their excitement as they dive deep into a new project. This book, like my workshops, is meant to teach you practical skills and to guide you through your first projects with wood. But beyond teaching you how to make your first gorgeous cutting board or bench, I also hope that this book will take you a step further on your journey, leading you to nurture your creative flow and to find inspiration all around you—in the woodshop and far beyond.

CHAPTER ONE

A WOMAN AND HER WOOD BENCH

Woodworking has been an essential part of our lives since the very beginning. Early humans used wood, one of nature's most beautiful resources, to create instruments for daily life. The first carpenters carved, cut, and finessed this hard yet malleable material to fashion tools and vessels for cooking and eating, to build shelter, and to create the first boats and vehicles for traveling across oceans and continents. Woodworking has a rich history, and it is an art form that reminds me of the human spirit: It's about growing, changing, learning, and expanding. Wood comes from the earth, and in our hands, through development and artistry, we transform it in ways that sustain life and offer beauty to the world.

My love affair with wood, like any relationship, has been a process. In the beginning, I was plagued by fears. Could I muster up the strength to be a confident woman in a field dominated by men? As a novice woodworker, would I be scoffed at for my still-developing skills? I've had to face these fears, and many more. I've had to get my hands dirty, just do it, and accept that failure would be an inevitable part of my journey.

One example: On my very first day at Anthropologie, I was tasked with making a sign for the checkout line in one of the stores. I eagerly accepted the assignment, knowing little to nothing about working with wood, aside from building frames for my paintings in college. As for power tools, I'd used a sander and a drill, and a small miter saw once but was not a master. That was about it. Still, I was feeling confident until I saw the huge power tool that I was also supposed to use to make this sign: their miter saw. I couldn't even get past turning off the safety. There were no instructions (this was before smartphones), and I was too embarrassed to ask anyone for help, so I pored over the saw, searching in vain for a release button. Eventually, feeling defeated, I rested my arms on the saw, and I felt it give a little. That little bit of pressure popped out the safety pin. Apparently, you just had to push down on the top of the saw handle. Propelled by a combination of laughter and rage, I quickly got to work. After wasting half a day trying to figure out that damn safety, I now had only one hour to cut and create the sign. The end result was terrible. I knew it. My boss knew it. But since it was my first day on the job, I got a lucky pass.

We've all had days like the one I'm describing. But from those moments of near or total failure, there is always some knowledge to be gained from the experience. With each failure, we end up just a bit wiser, and more graceful, than we were when starting out.

After my humbling saw snafu, through the nonstop projects and pressure of deadlines, I gradually began to feel comfortable in the woodshop. Eventually, when I was given the chance to work on displays that were made entirely from wood, my whole being would light up. I would completely lose myself in the materials. There was an excitement in creating without thinking, a blissful flood of inspiration. My creative third eye would open, blink a few times, and remain open, ready to receive. It felt as if my hands had found their home.

WOODWORKING TOOLS GUIDE

What I wouldn't have given for a handy little guide to woodworking tools when I was starting out! Below is a list of the tools I use most commonly in my workshop.

HAMMER: Used for driving nails into wood and for breaking objects apart. This is an essential tool to have in your arsenal.

CLAMP: A metal or wooden device that holds one object in place against another in a fixed position.

CHISEL: A carving tool that usually has a wooden handle and sharpened metal edge to carve or cut into wood.

ORBITAL SANDER: A power tool used to sand down or smooth surfaces. Sandpaper is attached to a round pad on the bottom of the sander, which vibrates in tiny circles in order to provide even smoothing.

MITER SAW: A tool used to make miter cuts, or crosscuts, into wood. It works by pulling a mounted circular saw blade down into the wood, causing a cut. Miter saws are used to make accurate angled cuts and come with a measurement base for a guide.

CIRCULAR SAW: A handheld power saw with a round blade that spins to make a cut.

POWER DRILL: A tool commonly used to drill holes or to drive screws into material.

NAIL GUN: A power tool used to drive nails into an object.

STRAIGHT EDGE/ GUIDE: A tool used to guide the saw in a straight line.

WOODWORKING SAFETY TIPS

Whenever operating a saw, drill, or sander, make sure to use the proper eye protection to cover your eyes from sawdust or any kind of material that could shoot back at you.

When sanding, use a respirator or wear a mask so that you don't inhale the sawdust. Also wear safety glasses to protect your eyes from anything the sander kicks free into the air.

Before operating the saw, first do your research and learn the appropriate safe hand placement. For best results, turn on the saw and get the blade running before you get it close to the wood to make a cut.

The more momentum the saw has, the better the cut.

Be mindful of your hand placement with every tool. Keep hands away from the saw blade, out of the way of the drill, and away from the sander.

If you have long hair, always tie it back before operating a power tool.

When carving or using a chisel, cut away from your body, not toward it.

Have fun and always be safe. And take it slow!

EXPLORING LUMBER:
FIND THE RIGHT WOOD TO WORK WITH

Once you have a particular project in mind, it's time to choose your materials. What kind of wood is best for your project? Is it a hardwood or a softwood? Begin with an online search. YouTube is a great resource when planning a project and sourcing information and materials. Another consideration is your budget. Common construction wood like pine tends to be cheaper, while rarer woods and most hardwoods, like walnut, are pricier. Have a clear idea of how much you want to spend on lumber before you head to the store. Once you know what you're looking for, jot down on a piece of paper the kind of wood you would like to purchase and how much of it you need, and then head out to a local lumberyard. The most important thing to remember once you head out to shop for lumber is that you shouldn't be afraid to empower yourself by asking questions!

Walking into a lumberyard or a hardware store as a beginner can be intimidating. But trust me, sourcing, testing, and scouting out lumber can be a lot of fun once you know the basics. The beauty of wood is in its imperfections. Each piece looks, feels, and behaves differently. That's why learning about each type of wood is so much fun.

AT THE LUMBERYARD

- Start by taking your time and looking around. Reach out and touch the different types of wood.
- Look closely at the wood grain, feel the density of the material. Smell the wood. Certain woods smell better than others. You'll find one that you love.

- Keep your list handy so that you can locate the types of wood you set out to find. Your first trip to the lumberyard can be a bit overwhelming, so it's good to stay organized.
- Pick out smaller pieces of wood that you can bring home to try, to see if you like working with a particular material.

   PRO TIP: *Browse the smaller "off-cut" section of a lumberyard. You'll find a plethora of scraps-samples at great discounts.*

- Hardwoods are more expensive, but they are often the most beautiful. Saving up for a special piece of walnut is always a treat.
- Choose three or four different types of wood to bring home with you.
- Don't overthink it. There really isn't a specific kind you *should* start with—just pick the ones you love.
- Congratulations on surviving the lumberyard! Now that the first trip is over with, you can go back with confidence.

MY FAVORITE TYPES OF WOOD

WALNUT: Hardwood. Commonly used for carving and woodworking, as well as in house finishes, such as flooring. Chocolate coloring, straight wood grain.

ASH: Hardwood. Commonly used for making frames, tools, and furniture. Light in color, straight-ish wood grain.

REDWOOD: Softwood. Commonly used for furniture, wood turning (which is a process of carving wood with a tool called a lathe), and musical instruments. Easy to work with, in colors that range from pinkish brown to reddish brown. The grain is primarily straight with some wavy irregular grains.

When we talk about "refining" lumber, we are referring to the process of cleaning up a piece of wood and getting it ready to work with. This includes sanding off the imperfections that are sometimes caused by storing, milling (a process in which logs are cut down into lumber), and/or transporting the wood. To start, select a piece of wood to work with and choose your sandpaper. Sandpaper has varying levels of grit based on how harshly or finely it will grade a piece of wood.

- Grit numbers 36 to 100: Apply these grades for heavier sanding jobs. You can use it for stripping away finishes such as paint or varnish and for evening out and shaping wood. If you're working with finer hardwoods, use caution as it may add scratches. Grit numbers 36 to 100 are great for removing bark, saw marks, and uneven levels that can appear during milling.
- Grit numbers 100 to 180: These development grades can be used for smoothing out your pieces, removing scratches or dents, and preparing the wood for finishing.
- Grit numbers 180 to 320: These grits are ideal for finishing your project, including removing any small imperfections, smoothing the surface, and sanding down different layers of finish.

SUPPLIES
60- and 220-grit sandpaper
Lumber of choice
Shop rag
Food-grade wood conditioner
Safety glasses

You'll start by hand-sanding the wood, using a coarse-grit sandpaper to work out any rough edges. I recommend using a 60-grit sandpaper so that you can shape the wood quickly without scratching it. The lower the number, the coarser the sandpaper is; the higher the number, the finer the grit is. You will progressively move toward a higher (finer) grit. Once you have evened out your wood and the finishing process has begun, 220-grit will finish the wood. Pay attention to how the wood interacts with your hands; notice where sanding is needed.

After you've smoothed out most of the rough edges, transition to the finer 220-grit sandpaper and continue to smooth out the piece.

Next, grab your shop rag and squeeze a generous amount of food-grade wood conditioner on the piece. Use a wood conditioner that contains food-grade mineral oil, meaning it's safe to use if you're making something that will touch food, like a bowl or a cutting board. Rub the conditioner in on both sides with the rag and then let the wood dry. The wood conditioner will bring out all the beautiful wood grain and quality of that specific type of wood.

Repeat with each piece of wood.

Now stand back and look at the wood you carefully chose and cared for. Did anything change through the conditioning process? Note the qualities that were different between the various types of wood you selected. Do you feel drawn to work with one type of wood in particular? Hopefully the answer is yes and you are excited about your next trip to the lumberyard!

TAKING MY SEAT AT THE WOOD BENCH

A pivotal moment for me on my journey to becoming a woodworker was buying my first saw, which was a Skilsaw compound miter saw. At the time, I was still working for Anthropologie, and it was perfect for my entry-level skills while also allowing some room to grow. It took me some time to save the money I'd need to buy it, and since I was living in a tiny San Francisco apartment, that huge power tool and I shared a bedroom. From there, I started creating my own abstract installations and artwork, securing my very first group show at a gallery in the Mission District in 2011.

That show was my entrée into the San Francisco arts community. At first, I was terrified. I felt like an impostor, like I didn't deserve to be part of the scene. But once I dove into my work and started attending shows, I met so many other incredible makers. The arts community in San Francisco is fantastic. Everyone supports one another and contributes to the growth of the entire community. There are some serious karmic vibes flying around. Maybe it's left over from the 1960s Free Love movement or the essence of counterculture infused in the city's roots.

It soon became impossible for me to balance a full-time job with my art, so I left Anthropologie. This was a tough call since I loved that job, but at the end of each working day, after pouring myself into my projects at Anthropologie, I would come home too exhausted to put the time into my own art. I still needed to pay my rent, so I took a waitressing job at a restaurant near my house that could offer me flexibility and wouldn't drain my creative energy.

Once I had the energetic space for my art and woodworking to develop, I needed a physical space, other than my tiny apartment, to work on my projects. So my saw and I soon began squatting in the basement of my apartment building, unbeknownst to my landlord. We took over a 5 × 10-foot storage space, and just like that, my illegal workshop was up and running! I finally had a place to stash all my lumber and my growing collection of tools. Everything was going swimmingly until a washing-machine leak outed my operation, and the landlord kicked me (and my saw) out of the space. But I kept honing my craft, waiting tables at night to fund my creativity, and eventually I had the resources to move into a real shared studio space.

After three years of working in my studio by day and waiting tables at night, a little voice started telling me that it was time to devote myself 100 percent to my craft. I was gaining traction with art shows, my sales had picked up, and my commissioned orders were increasing to a point that was unmanageable while working another job. All signs pointed to making this my full-time gig. But fear was holding me back. It was like standing in the surf, wading into the ocean, and trying to decide whether to struggle against the waves as they hit me or to dive under and come out on the other side swimming. My restaurant job was my security blanket, and letting go of it was a huge leap of faith. But I finally did it, and from that moment forward, my art became the center of my life and carried the responsibility of sustaining me. Yes, I was liberated from a "real" job, but that presented a whole new set of challenges. Projects and commissions were stacking up and it felt like there simply were not enough hours in the day to get it all done. Plus, at twenty-six years old, having started my own business, I was now the one solely responsible for organizing, scheduling, and prioritizing everything. There was no one to do those things for me. The feeling of hustle has never left me, and I'm always chasing bigger projects and pushing myself to grow. The hustle is what led me to find my way to a bright, light, airy Oakland studio where I'm currently doing my best work ever. I still pinch myself every time I walk in, turn on one of my many saws, and think about how far I've come.

WOODEN COASTERS

DIFFICULTY LEVEL: BEGINNER

Making coasters is one of my favorite projects. They are useful for your own home and great to give as gifts. Since I do a lot of entertaining in my home and I have a good amount of wood furniture, protecting it is very important. I always leave coasters on the table to remind me to use them and to have them ready for my guests.

SUPPLIES

Two 1 x 4 x 24-inch pieces of lumber

Measuring tape

Pencil

60- and 220-grit sandpaper for an orbital sander

Food-grade wood conditioner

Shop rag

Safety glasses

Respirator

TOOLS

Miter saw

Orbital sander

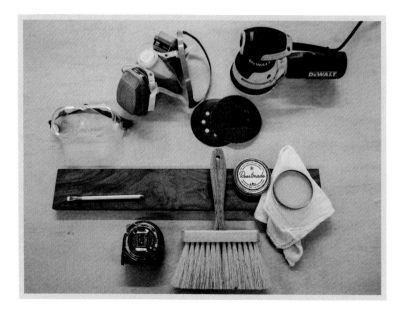

STEP ONE: CHOOSE THE LUMBER

For this project, I am working with walnut, but you can use any variety that you are drawn to.

STEP TWO: MEASURE THE SIZE OF THE COASTERS

Measure and draw out one 4 × 4-inch square. Only draw one square out at a time, as the saw blade will take away around ⅛ inch with each cut.

STEP THREE: CUT THE WOOD

Place the lumber on the saw, holding with one hand the end you are not cutting to steady the wood. Before you cut the piece make sure you are cutting on the side of the line you will not be using.

Start the saw before bringing the blade close to the wood. Pull down the handle of the blade and cut the first edge of your first coaster.

Repeat this motion until you have cut out your first square. Trace your first square on the next piece of lumber and repeat the cutting steps.

Repeat five to seven times to make a full set of coasters.

STEP FOUR: SAND THE COASTERS

Attach the 60-grit sandpaper to your orbital sander. You will work upward to finer sandpaper. Hold down your piece of wood with one hand while you sand with the other, smoothing out the imperfections and rough-cut lines. Remove the sandpaper from the sander and replace it with the softer 220-grit sandpaper. Smooth out your wood with the sander and make it soft to the touch (no splinters). Do this to both sides of all the coasters.

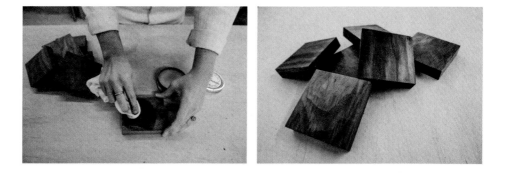

STEP FIVE: FINISH THE COASTERS

Now that your sanding is complete, it is time to condition and protect the wood. Pour a quarter-size dollop of the wood conditioner onto one side of each coaster. Rub the conditioner into the wood with the rag, getting into all the grain and along the edges. Let sit for 20 minutes and then flip and do the other side.

Repeat this process twice more. Three coats will "season" the coasters.

SAFETY TIPS

Make sure you are comfortable using both a miter saw and a sander.

If you have long hair, tie it back.

Always wear the proper safety glasses and respirator.

Keep fingers away from the saw blade and sander.

INTO THE GRAIN

There's just something about wood. It's an imperfect material with cracks, knots, and irregularities. I find that by working with wood, with all its imperfections and inconsistencies, I can also tackle my own. I get lost and then find myself in the swirling labyrinths of the

wood grain, and this hard yet flexible material plucked from nature has become my teacher as I learn to love my own flaws.

Each type of wood is so unique, distinct in its hue, texture, direction of the grain, and the way it responds when you cut it. Early on in my woodworking career, I was drawn to reclaimed lumber. I loved pulling its existing character and story into my work, because it had already lived a life, or even multiple lives, before we crossed paths. I would put a lot of care into restoring the old, discarded wood. At the same time, I was also beginning to write a new story for myself, stripping away old programming, fears, and beliefs that weren't serving me anymore.

The type of wood that I choose to work with often reflects my personal journey, and the more time I have spent working on myself alongside my craft, the more I have begun to crave clean lines, minimalist designs, and calming earth tones. Moving away from reclaimed lumber made sense, and that's when redwood, my new favorite, appeared. Redwood became my preferred material because it is soft, easy to manipulate, resistant to rot, and lightweight without compromising its strength. Plus, it is sustainably farmed, which gets a big green thumbs-up from me. The wood, in warm shades of beet, blond, and tangerine, also maintains a unique pattern from the heartwood (center of the tree) to the sapwood (outer edge) that feels like magic in the way it can look like water or sometimes even like hair. As I got to know redwood, I became mesmerized with its beauty, studying the ripples and ribbons within each slab and allowing its unique variations to guide my work.

When I study the grain and growth rings of the wood I'm using, I am reminded that growth is inevitable, but it takes time. It's not something that happens overnight, but when you look back at the center of the tree, you can see how far it's come.

A FIELD GUIDE TO COMMON HARDWOODS AND SOFTWOODS

COMMON WOOD TYPES

HARDWOOD: Most hardwoods, which include alder, mahogany, maple, oak, teak, and walnut, have a higher density than softwoods. Hardwoods grow at a slower rate than softwoods. A fun fact about hardwoods is that most of them reproduce through the pollination of their flowers, and the wood has pores.

SOFTWOOD: Softwoods, including cedar, fir, white oak, ponderosa pine, and redwood, are not always softer, but they are for the most part less dense than hardwood trees. Softwood trees have a faster growth rate and they reproduce through seeds. Softwood is the primary source of construction lumber.

HEARTWOOD: Literally the heart of the tree, heartwood is the center, where growth, and the tree's life, starts. Heartwood usually is much darker, changes in color over time, and is resistant to rot.

SAPWOOD: Sapwood is younger wood, from the outer rings of the tree, between the heartwood and the bark. It is the tree's living wood and where sap flows. Its job is to bring water to the rest of the tree. A tree always begins as sapwood and works its way outward.

WOOD FROM DIFFERENT TYPES OF TREES

ACACIA

ACACIA: Acacia is a hardwood native to Australia and Africa, golden rust in color and with a wavy grain. It is resistant to bugs and rot and is most commonly used for furniture, bowls, canoes, and carving.

ALDER

ALDER: The most abundant hardwood in the northwestern United States, alder has a straighter grain with a light tan to reddish color. It is most commonly used for furniture, cabinets, musical instruments, and plywood.

ASH

ASH: Ash is a soft hardwood whose heartwood is medium brown and sapwood is light brown. It has a straight wood grain and is most commonly used for flooring and baseball bats as well as projects that require the wood to be steamed and bent.

BIRCH

BIRCH: A hardwood with reddish-brown to yellow heartwood and white sapwood, birch has a straight to slightly wavy wood grain. It is most commonly used for plywood, trim, and objects turned on a lathe.

CEDAR

CEDAR: Cedar is a softwood with a light red heartwood and white sapwood. The wood grain is straight with little variation. It is most commonly used for construction lumber, boats, and carving.

CHERRY

CHERRY: A hardwood with a deep golden-brown color and a straight and wavy wood grain, cherry is also susceptible to insects. It is most commonly used for furniture, instruments, carving, and cabinetry.

CHESTNUT

CHESTNUT: Chestnut is a hardwood with a light to medium brown heartwood that darkens; its sapwood is light brown. The grain can be straight or spiral. It is most commonly used for flooring.

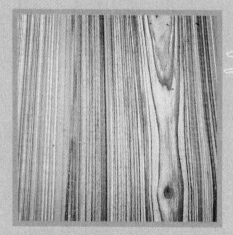

CYPRESS: A softwood with light brown heartwood, white sapwood, and a straight grain, cypress is most commonly used in boatbuilding, trim, and exterior lumber.

CYPRESS

DOUGLAS FIR: Douglas fir is a softwood that is light brown, yellow, and red in color. The grain is straight and wavy. It is most commonly used for construction lumber.

DOUGLAS FIR

ELM: There are many different types of elm. Rock elm, cedar elm, and winged elm are all hardwoods, while American elm, English elm, and red elm are softwoods. English elm has a light reddish-brown heartwood and pale sapwood. The grain is interlocked and wavy. It is most commonly used for baskets, furniture, and archery bows.

ENGLISH ELM

ENGLISH WALNUT

ENGLISH WALNUT: English walnut is a hardwood. Its heartwood can be a dark chocolate brown to a lighter brown with dark streaks ranging from purple to red to gray; the sapwood is white. The wood grain is straight but can have irregular wavy and curly grains. It is most commonly used for fine woodworking, furniture, and cutting boards.

MAPLE

HARD MAPLE: Hard maple is a hardwood with dark reddish-brown heartwood and a cream sapwood. The grain is wavy and sometimes straight. It is most commonly used for butcher blocks, cutting boards, flooring, worktables, and turned objects.

MAHOGANY

MAHOGANY: A dark reddish hardwood that darkens with age, mahogany has a beautiful, rich straight grain. It is resistant to rot and most commonly used for furniture and musical instruments.

PONDEROSA

PONDEROSA PINE: A softwood with red-brown heartwood, white sapwood, and a straight grain, Ponderosa pine is most commonly used as a building material.

POPLAR

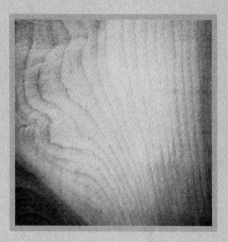

POPLAR: Poplar is a hardwood whose heartwood is creamy yellow in color while the sapwood is a paler yellow. The grain is uniform and straight. It is most commonly used for building pallets, plywood, and furniture.

REDWOOD: Redwood is a softwood with heartwood that ranges from pinkish brown to dark deep reddish brown. Its sapwood is clear and defined by light yellow coloring. The grain is straight and can be wavy and irregular. It is most commonly used for construction materials, decks, outdoor furniture, musical instruments, and furniture.

REDWOOD

SPRUCE

SPRUCE: Spruce is a softwood with heartwood that is yellow and brown and sapwood that is yellow and white. The grain is straight. It is most commonly used for heavy construction, railroad ties, bridges, beams, and structural construction.

TEAK: Teak is a hardwood that is rich golden brown to medium brown in the heartwood and slightly lighter toward the sapwood. The grain is straight but can vary with wavy interlocked grains. It is most commonly used for furniture, exterior structural construction, boatbuilding, turning, and carving.

TEAK

WHITE OAK

WHITE OAK: A light to medium brown softwood with a straight wood grain, white oak is also rot resistant. It is most commonly used for cabinetry, boatbuilding, barrels, and furniture.

NESTING CUTTING BOARDS

DIFFICULTY LEVEL: BEGINNER

I have a collection of cutting boards at home, some that I have made, and a few that I have been gifted. I love having a pile of them around the house. From kitchen prep, to serving, to entertaining they have so many uses! I love making a giant spread, piling a cutting board high with all the goodies and inviting friends over for evening snacks and drinks. Wooden cutting boards also travel well for picnics and look great displayed in the kitchen.

SUPPLIES

Measuring tape
Pencil
One 2 x 12 x 36-inch or larger piece of lumber
60- and 220-grit sandpaper for an orbital sander
Food-grade wood conditioner
Shop rag
Safety glasses
Respirator

TOOLS

Miter saw
Orbital sander

STEP ONE: CHOOSE THE LUMBER

Hardwood is the best choice for this project, since cutting boards tend to take a beating. I've chosen walnut, but you can choose a variety of hardwoods for this project.

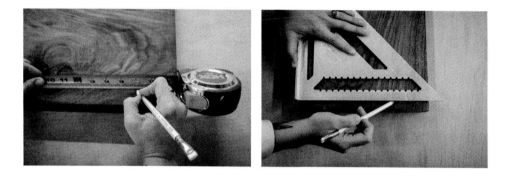

STEP TWO: MEASURE THE SIZE OF YOUR CUTTING BOARDS

We'll make two rectangular boards, one slightly bigger than the other.

Measure and draw out a 12 × 16-inch rectangle. That will be your first cut. You will then measure a 10 × 14-inch rectangle on the piece that is left from your first cut and cut that to size.

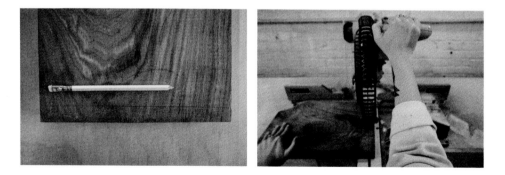

STEP THREE: CUT THE WOOD

Place the lumber on the saw, holding with one hand the end you are not cutting to steady the wood. Before you cut the piece, make sure you are cutting on the side of the line you will not be using.

Start the saw before bringing the blade close to the wood. Pull down the blade and cut the first edge of your first cutting board. Repeat this motion until you have cut out your first rectangle. Follow the same steps for the next cutting board.

STEP FOUR: SAND THE CUTTING BOARDS

Attach the 60-grit sandpaper to your orbital sander. You will work upward to finer sandpaper. Hold down your piece of wood with one hand while you sand with the other. Smooth out the imperfections and rough-cut lines. Remove the sandpaper and replace it with the softer 220-grit sandpaper. Smooth out your wood with the sander and make it soft to the touch (no splinters). Do this to both sides of both cutting boards.

STEP FIVE: FINISH THE CUTTING BOARDS

Now that your sanding is complete, it is time to condition and protect the wood. Pour a quarter-size dollop of the wood conditioner onto one side of each cutting board, adding more as you go. Try not to put on too much at first; it's always easier to add than to take away. Rub the conditioner into the wood with the rag, getting into all the grain and along the edges. Let sit for 20 minutes and then flip and do the other side.

Repeat this process twice more to properly season the boards a total of three times. To keep your boards conditioned, repeat this process from time to time when the wood seems to be drying out.

SAFETY TIPS

Make sure you are comfortable using both a miter saw and sander.

If you have long hair, tie it back.

Always wear the proper safety glasses and respirator.

Keep fingers away from the saw blade and sander.

WHERE MY STYLE WAS BORN

The specific style that characterizes my work is deeply inspired by the desert settings of the Southwest. I draw on the bold shapes, the textures, the ebbs and flows, and the feelings of stillness and calm inherent in these landscapes to fuel my work. Joshua Tree National Park is one of my favorite places on earth, and the more time that I spend there, the more I find myself incorporating desert tones into my work. I love returning to this incredibly special, meditative spot again and again, and I find myself captivated by its rugged terrain and warm, natural hues. Quiet and monochromatic, like a dust storm that covers everything in a fine coat of beige.

NATURAL DYE BANDANAS WITH WOOD IN COLLABORATION WITH APPRVL

DIFFICULTY LEVEL: BEGINNER

While most of my time is spent at my wood bench, I wouldn't be where I am today without a crew of people who supported my dreams and helped show me the way. I've made the intentional choice to surround myself with creative people whom I admire and who hustle and work toward their goals in much the way that I do. My community is made up of fearless and creative women and men from a variety of disciplines who are pushing the boundaries of what's creatively possible. Their action and conviction inspire me to work harder.

Collaboration is such an important part of what I do and I'm always excited to join creative forces with people I admire. That's why I partnered up with my dear friend Megan Mussari, who founded Apprvl, a brand that creates handmade and hand-dyed textiles out of New York City. Beyond textiles, she teaches workshops and sells DIY kits that you can use to make your own naturally dyed products at home. And that's exactly what we're going to do! Her bandanas are my favorite and together we are going to teach you how to dye them with wood.

Pot large enough to hold
fabric and water

1 tablespoon soda ash

2 cotton bandanas

6 to 8 tablespoons aluminum
acetate

7 or 8 tablespoons cutch dye
extract

Liquid measuring cup or
other small container, for
dissolving dye. A metal pot is
best.

Rubber bands (optional)

GETTING STARTED

Natural dyes like those derived from wood should only be used
on natural fibers. We recommend using bandanas that are 100%
cotton. (Following these instructions on silk, wool, or linen may yield
different results; synthetic fibers like polyester, nylon, and rayon will
not hold colors from natural sources.)

This recipe will dye two matching bandanas, one for you and one for
a friend. I've been known to outfit my furry friend, Jack, in his own.

STEP ONE: SCOUR THE FABRIC

Scouring is an important first step in treating the fabric, since most fabrics have a finish on them. This will ensure that the fibers will be able to easily absorb the mordants and dyes. We prefer scouring with soda ash, which is available at most art stores. If you don't have access to soda ash, you can prewash the bandanas with regular detergent in hot water.

SODA ASH SCOUR

Heat water to 140°F in a pot large enough for your fabrics to move around freely and not be too crumpled up. Add the soda ash and stir until dissolved. Add the fabrics and keep water temperature at around 140°F for 30 minutes. Rinse with cool water.

STEP TWO: APPLY THE MORDANTING TREATMENT

Natural dyes need the help of mordants, or fixatives, which help fibers retain long-lasting deep color. Our mordant of choice is aluminum acetate when working with cotton.

MORDANTING

Heat a large pot of water to 110°F (you do not need to let the water come to a boil first). Add the aluminum acetate and stir to dissolve.

Add the fabric and leave in the pot for 45 to 60 minutes, stirring occasionally and keeping the water at the same temperature.

Rinse with cool water and keep the fabric wet for the dying process.

STEP THREE: DYE THE BANDANA

Our favorite wood dye is cutch dye extract. It comes from the heartwood of the acacia tree and it can generate light caramel tans to rich mahogany browns depending on how long you let the material sit in the dye bath. Longer times yield darker colors. For a nice medium camel color, we will use about 7 tablespoons of cutch extract.

Put the cutch extract in the measuring cup and add a cup of hot water. Stir to dissolve before introducing it to the larger pot of water that you will dye in. Dissolving the extract first prevents clumping during the dyeing process. Once the dye is dissolved and added to the large pot, place the wet bandanas into the pot and simmer over low heat, stirring occasionally. You want to make sure that there are no air bubbles hiding in your bandanas, which may cause uneven dying. You can also play around with binding the fabrics with rubber bands for a patterned shibori look.

Cutch makes a beautiful color when it is left to simmer for a few hours. Check on the fabrics every 20 minutes or so. Once you have reached your desired color, remove the bandanas and let them sit in the sink for a few minutes before rinsing them in room-temperature water.

Hang the bandanas to dry or place them in a dryer on a low setting.

When washing your bandanas in the future, it's best to hand-wash with a gentle detergent to keep that rich color going strong.

CHAPTER TWO

FINDING YOUR CREATIVE CALLING

When you observe someone deep in their creative process from the outside, it may all look simple. But tapping into your own creativity isn't always easy. It's important to keep in mind that whether or not you consider yourself an artist, creative energy is always available to you somewhere below the surface. You just have to be willing to look for it. In my experience, the push to create comes and goes. Some days everything feels like a struggle in the studio. Other days hours fly by before I even think to step away from the workbench. What can you do to stoke the fire when you're feeling creatively stuck? There are a few tricks I've picked up over the years to tap into that urge to create and to get the process started.

First, acknowledge that you have a creative drive. There is a creative force inside of you that's desperate to get out. Say hello to it. Second, the most important part, nurture your creativity. Many of us simply don't take the time to do this. Third, embrace creative failure. Not every project that you embark on, especially at first, is going to turn out the way you envision it. And that's okay. It's all part of the process. I failed miserably many times in my early days. The more comfortable you get with making bad art, the more creative risks you'll be willing to take.

The key is to let your creative energy flow and to see where it takes you. Don't limit yourself. Listen to your intuition for ideas. Follow your inspiration. Think about colors, textures, shapes, and movements that excite you. Get your hands dirty. Try something new. What's the worst thing that could happen? You fail. The best? You give a voice to a part of yourself that you never knew existed.

DIY

BLANKET LADDER

DIFFICULTY LEVEL: MODERATE

I'm constantly updating the decor in my house because I love changing things up and keeping them fresh. So being able to make furniture or home accent pieces myself is a major plus! As an avid textile collector living in a small space, I'm always looking for creative ways to store and show off my wares. Enter this versatile 7-foot-tall blanket ladder. This project's value is twofold: It creates storage for your soft goods while adding a decorative touch to your home.

SUPPLIES

Measuring tape

Pencil

Masking or painters' tape

Two 1½-inch x 8-foot pine hand rail dowels

Five 1¼-inch x 4-foot pine round wood dowels

60-grit sandpaper

Wood glue

Shop rags

Polycrylic wood finish

Safety glasses

Gloves

TOOLS

Miter saw

Drill with 1⅛-inch spade drill bit

6-foot pipe clamps

Hammer

STEP ONE: CUT THE HAND RAIL DOWELS

Using your miter saw, cut both hand rail dowels to 84 inches long.

STEP TWO: CUT THE ROUND DOWELS

Measure and mark your round dowels at 30 inches, 28½ inches, 27 inches, 25½ inches, 24 inches, and 22½ inches and make the cuts. This will make your blanket ladder 84 inches tall, 32 inches wide at the base, and 25½ inches wide at the top.

STEP THREE: PREP THE HAND RAILS FOR DRILLING

Mark the side pieces (the hand rails) for your drill holes, which will
be where your dowels will fit in. Measure 12 inches down from the
top of the first side piece and draw a line. Repeat every 12 inches until
you have six lines. After your lines are drawn, measure the center of
the hand rail on the flat side (⅝ inch) and mark it with an X. This is
where you will drill your hole.

STEP FOUR: DRILL THE WOOD

Mark the spade drill bit with a piece of tape at ½ inch from the tip
of the bit. This will give you a marker for how deep to drill your hole,
ensuring that you will not drill all the way through the wood. Attach
your spade bit to the drill. Clamp down each hand rail. Place the bit
in the center of the X that you have made six times on each side of
your hand rail. Drill until the tape is level with the top of the wood.
Continue until all six holes on each hand rail have been drilled.

STEP FIVE: SAND THE WOOD

Sand by hand any rough edges on the wood you have just cut, including the dowels, hand rails, and drill holes.

STEP SIX: ASSEMBLE THE BLANKET LADDER

Lay out the hand rails next to one another, hole side up. Fill the holes with a pea-size amount of wood glue. Fit the dowels into the holes and lightly hammer them into place on both sides. Wipe away any extra glue with a rag.

Clamp the ladder by tightening your clamps on the wood. Make sure to tighten evenly, going back and forth until you see a little bead of glue coming from where you placed the dowel into the hole. Do not overtighten. Wipe away the bead of glue. Let the glue around the dowels dry for at least an hour.

STEP SEVEN: FINISH THE WOOD

Pour wood finish onto a clean rag and work it into the wood. Apply two coats. Let dry overnight. All done!

SAFETY TIPS

Make sure you are comfortable using a miter saw and drill.

If you have long hair, tie it back.

Always wear the proper safety glasses.

Keep fingers away from the saw blade and drill bit.

SOURCING YOUR CREATIVITY

All this talk of creativity, but where do you begin? It's as simple as being more present and paying more attention to the natural world around you.

At Anthropologie, my window installations would always reflect the seasons. A big part of what I created was influenced by what I saw on the train from San Francisco to Palo Alto on my way into the studio. The colors and textures I used tended to mirror what I saw when I looked out the window watching the world go by. During the summer, my displays would reflect the vibrant sun-soaked landscape and bright blue skies. In the winter, the naked trees would inspire me to incorporate lots of wool and muted fall colors in my designs.

When you're truly present, you begin seeing the world through fresh eyes. Elements in your environment that were always there but that you may not have noticed before will begin to emerge. Living in Oakland, my favorite way to do this exercise is to take a drive to the ocean. Sitting there and watching the waves rise and fall, and observing the repetition of their shapes and texture, is always inspiring to me. Once I've taken it all in, I always return to the shop with a new energy and new ideas about the kind of motion and shapes that I can incorporate into my work.

CREATIVE SOURCING IN THE HIGH DESERT

While being open to inspiration in your daily routine is a good start, getting away from home can introduce a fresh perspective and ignite new creative energy. One of my favorite places for refreshing my creative practice is Joshua Tree National Park in southeastern California, where I travel several times a year for a creative recharge. The high desert has always been a place of inspiration for me. There is a magic in the seemingly barren landscape, with the monochromatic earth and plants providing a perfect backdrop to the stunning pink sunsets and sunrises. There are so many aspects of Joshua Tree that keep me yearning to return. I feel that every time I visit I am drawn to something different, and I cling to these moments of inspiration when I am back in the woodshop making my art. Joshua Tree is my creative source, but this exercise can be done in any natural environment that you find beautiful and calming—even at your local park or beach.

To get the full benefits of this creative exercise, I recommend that you visit your chosen environment twice, once in the morning and once at sunset. Remember to pay close attention to the changes you observe: changes in temperature, in the shadows that shift with the movement of the sun, in the colors that differ from sunrise to sunset. Take note of the energy you feel from the landscape as the day moves from morning to afternoon to night.

SUPPLIES

Small notebook   Pen or pencil

STEP ONE: GROUND YOURSELF

Before you begin, find a comfortable spot indoors and take a moment to ground yourself. Stand up straight and plant both feet firmly on the ground. Take three deep breaths, allowing the air to fill your lungs completely, and then exhale. Step outside and do the same—three deep breaths.

STEP TWO: WANDER

Commit to at least 30 minutes of mindfully wandering around in nature. Grab your writing utensil and notebook to document what you're experiencing. Notice the weather, the clouds, the breeze, the smells, and the sounds. Are there plants around? Pay attention to the texture of the ground beneath your feet. What colors catch your eye? Take a moment to jot down what you see, hear, smell, and feel around you. Hunt for specifics, from a beautifully shaped stone, to a feather, to a discarded item that may have ended up there accidentally. Whatever inspires you. If you're not in a national park or on someone's private property, go ahead and collect a few items to take with you.

Once you've spent some time taking in the landscape, return home and place everything you've collected in front of you. What attracted you to those things? What textures and colors were you drawn to? Write down everything. This inspired information is now yours to bring back into your creative practice and access on demand. The more you do this, the more creative reserves you'll have stored up for a rainy day.

FINDING YOUR PERSONAL AESTHETIC

Whether you're sourcing inspiration from your surroundings or from other talented artists and makers, there are endless opportunities to take what you have stored up and use it to create your own personal style. But keep in mind that it takes time to develop an aesthetic. It took me years to develop the style I have now. When I first began

working with wood, I was deeply inspired by the ebb and flow of the sea. The ocean felt both new and old, wild and wise, and this energy informed my aesthetic. I would never leave the beach empty handed; I was always collecting things I could repurpose in my projects.

Driftwood was one of my favorites and it has served many purposes in my house, including, most recently, as sun-bleached dowels for hanging tapestries on my wall.

In my early work, I also used a lot of reclaimed wood. Any old piece of lumber I could get my hands on, I would try to make something out of it. The pieces I created during this period were flawed, raw, not perfectly cut or matched and I absolutely loved them. I'd spend hours in the shop re-creating the feeling of being in front of the ocean, and as a result, this aesthetic flowed through all areas of my life.

As a creative, your aesthetic will naturally be informed by the materials that you choose to work with. These materials should align with what you value, where you find beauty, and what sits right with your soul. It has always been important to me to know that I am not harming the environment in my creative pursuits, and all the lumber that I use today is sustainably sourced.

Your aesthetic will likely shift and adapt with you over time, but it's all about incorporating elements that move you into your personal space and craft—items as simple as a stick from the beach.

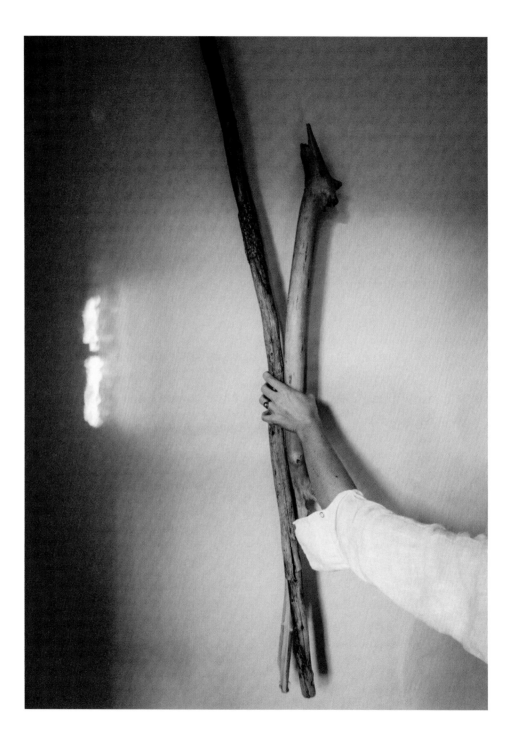

WALKING-STICK TAPESTRY

SUPPLIES

Tapestry or fabric

Measuring tape

Driftwood or fallen branch
measuring 10 inches longer
than width of tapestry

60-grit sandpaper

Pencil

Two hooks

Level

One Phillips head 2-inch
screw

TOOLS

Drill with Phillips bit

STEP ONE: SOURCE THE DRIFTWOOD

Find a tapestry or piece of fabric that you would like to hang on the
wall. Measure the length of the tapestry. Make a trip to the beach or
go on a hike to find a piece of driftwood or a fallen branch. Choose
a piece of wood that is at least 10 inches longer than your tapestry.
(Choose several pieces if you want to build a collection to use around
the house for various projects.) Remove any loose bark from your
wood, smooth it out with sandpaper by hand, and set it in the sun to
dry if it is damp.

STEP TWO: MEASURE AND MARK

With a pencil, mark the edges of where your tapestry will hit on your
piece of wood. Make a small mark 3 inches from the edge of the piece
of wood on both sides. That is where your tapestry stick will sit on
the hooks.

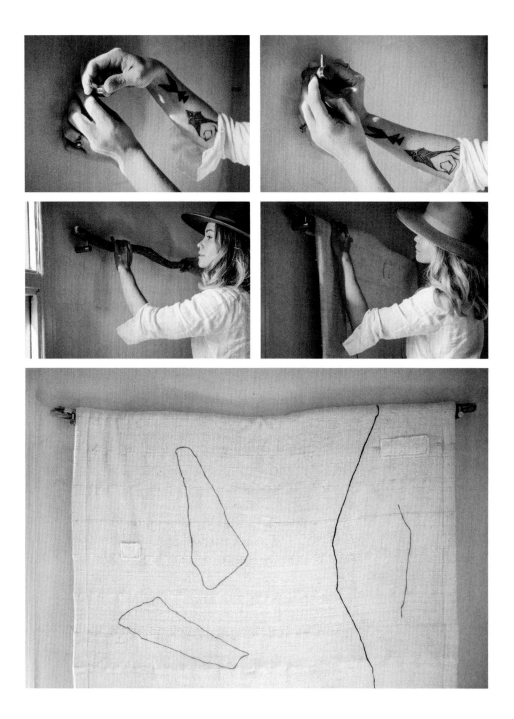

STEP THREE: INSTALL THE HOOKS

Measure the length of your piece of wood. Then measure the length of your tapestry, which will drape over your piece of wood. Keep in mind that your tapestry will need to hang over your piece of wood far enough to keep it in place, at least 1 foot. With those measurements in mind, assess the wall where you are going to hang your tapestry. You don't want your tapestry to touch the floor when it is hanging, so make sure that the hooks securing your tapestry to the wall are positioned so that your tapestry has around 1 foot of clearance from the floor and at least 1 foot of clearance from the ceiling. Mark a light X on the wall to indicate how high the hooks need to be placed.

Once you have decided on the height measurement, determine where your hooks need to be installed width-wise by measuring the length of the piece of wood where your pencil marks have been drawn (3 inches from either end). This marks the distance that will need to be placed between the hooks on the wall. To ensure the hooks are level, measure from the ground up to your desired height for each hook and make a mark. Double-check your work: Measure the distance between your two marks to make sure it is the same as the marks on your wood.

Screw the hooks into the wall: Start with your drill and 2-inch screw. We are going to create a small hole that will make it easier for the hook to be twisted in. Drill the screw into the mark you made for the hook, going slowly and only drilling in ⅓ of the screw before removing it. Repeat for the other hook placement mark. After your guide holes are made, twist in your hooks. Place the wood on the hooks. Use the level to ensure the wood is straight.

STEP FOUR: DRAPE

Drape the tapestry over the wood and enjoy your new piece of nature-inspired art!

SAFETY TIPS

Make sure you are comfortable using a drill.

If you have long hair, tie it back.

Keep fingers away from the drill.

As we grow and change, move to new places and try new things, we evolve. Accordingly, so does our creative library. In a rut? Travel. Get outside and see something new. You don't need to go far; you just need to get out of your usual routine and your comfort zone. Road trips or even quick day trips to a favorite destination can provide a fresh perspective. Following is an adventurous DIY project that's quick, easy, and ends in a picnic!

DESERT PICNIC TABLE AND SEATS: AN EASY, ON-THE-GO POP-UP PICNIC!

DIFFICULTY LEVEL: MODERATE

SUPPLIES

One 2 x 4-foot piece of precut pine plywood (½ inch or ¾ inch thickness will do)

One Burro Brand 29-inch contractor sawhorse

Measuring tape

Pencil

2-inch star flat-head wood deck screws

Two Burro Brand 24-inch contractor sawhorses

Picnic supplies, including yummy food, wine, blankets, napkins, etc.

Safety glasses

TOOL

Drill with star bit

STEP ONE: SOURCE THE MATERIALS

For this project, you'll be able to find everything you need in one fell swoop at a Home Depot or Lowe's. First, you'll need your tabletop. Head to the precut lumber aisle and look for a 2 × 4-foot pine top. Next, you'll want to grab the Burro Brand sawhorses, a 29-inch sawhorse for the table and two 24-inch ones for the seats. Finally, grab a box of 2-inch star flat-head wood deck screws and you're good to go!

STEP TWO: ASSEMBLE THE TABLE

Place your tabletop on the 29-inch sawhorse so that the distance between the overhanging tabletop to the sawhorse is the same on both ends and the tabletop is centered. Once you have the top positioned, measure and mark the center of the pine top and drill one screw into the sawhorse. Next, measure 6 inches to the right and left of that center screw, mark the placement, and drill in the second and third screws.

Now your tabletop is nice and secure! The two 24-inch sawhorses will serve as the bench seats for the table you just made.

STEP THREE: PREP THE PICNIC

Gather your picnic supplies and pack them all up.

STEP FOUR: ENJOY!

SAFETY TIPS

Make sure you are comfortable using a drill.

Always wear the proper safety glasses.

Keep fingers away from the drill bit.

MY GUIDE TO TRAVEL
FOR CREATIVE INSPIRATION

Travel has always provided me with endless inspiration. Varying landscapes, colors, and climates all offer different connections to the earth and ways to tap into the creative process. I've put together the following guide to the places that bring me the most inspiration so that you can enjoy them, too, drawing all that you can from our glorious Mother Earth.

BIG SUR

This is a stunning sliver of the California coast that is not to be missed. Every single time I venture here, the cliffs that plunge into the bright blue sea take my breath away. There is a magic in this landscape that calls me back no matter the season, from summer, when the sun shines over the endless coastline, to winter, with its glorious fog and the fierce ocean breaking over the cliffs below.

DON'T MISS

BIXBY CANYON BRIDGE: This bridge dates back to 1932, and perched at 260 feet above the canyon, it's one of the highest bridges in the world. Merging the gap between Carmel and San Luis Obispo, it's as functional as it is beautiful, making transportation easier from north to south. The simplicity in its design melds perfectly into the bend of the natural coastline. This bridge is a work of art.

THE HENRY MILLER LIBRARY: This is a nonprofit that focuses on literary arts and cultural artist contributions. Tucked off Highway 1, it was built by Emil White, who was Henry Miller's best friend in the 1960s. Miller was known for being a major influence in the Beat Generation of American writers, which produced Jack Kerouac. The library even has live music on occasion—some of my favorites who have played there are Patti Smith, Flaming Lips, and Father John Misty. You can get cozy and read a book from the library's curated selection or just hang out and catch the vibe.

MCWAY FALLS: Although you'll have to battle some tourists, this view is completely worth it, and at sunset, especially, it will take your breath away. The 80-foot waterfall is not to be missed, especially if it's your first time in Big Sur. The falls flow year-round from McWay Creek, crashing onto the beach below and finally into the Pacific Ocean.

BIG SUR HIKING

ANDREW MOLERA LOOP: An all-day 9-mile hike, this loop offers stunning coastal views and access to many remote beaches that often you can have all to yourself.

EWOLDSEN TRAIL: This 4.5-mile hike with sprawling redwood groves and endless ocean vistas provides the best of both worlds in a single destination.

PLACES TO STAY

VENTANA BIG SUR: This luxurious resort makes you feel right at home from the moment you enter the stunning property. With views of the redwoods and the endless ocean, you'll never want to leave. Designed with elegant simplicity, there are so many beautiful wooden touches and so much amazing furniture. The bathhouse is my favorite part of the property, where you can watch the sun set or stargaze. Both the men's and women's sides of the bathhouse have an open-air hot tub. Men and women can enjoy the tubs on their separate sides in the nude or meet up at a tub in the middle with swimsuits for co-ed relaxing. Some of the rooms have their own private outdoor hot tub, which is beyond romantic and quite a spectacular way to watch the night sky.

VENTANA CAMPING: Camp among the giant redwoods! The Ventana property offers both drive-up camping and, for a more luxe experience, glamping. It's the perfect spot to enjoy all the outdoor glory of Big Sur.

Truth be told, the high desert is my biggest inspiration. It's where my art was born and where I keep returning to create new work. I am eternally in awe of the landscapes, the life that somehow thrives in these climates, the sunrise, the sunsets, and every little bit of time in between.

California

JOSHUA TREE NATIONAL PARK

DON'T MISS

CHOLLA CACTUS GARDEN: The Cholla Cactus Garden is one of my favorite spots in Joshua Tree. There are thousands of cholla cacti covering the area, and at just the right time of day the sun hits their spines and makes them look like they are glowing—picture a field of warm rays of light. It's truly a sight to behold. Do be careful around these pretty plants, though. They're nicknamed "jumping cholla" for a reason. Getting too close to these beauties can result in a painful spine or two in your skin.

HIDDEN VALLEY NATURE TRAIL: The Hidden Valley Nature Trail is a beginner's hike, welcoming you into the captivating vastness of the park. Traverse the 1-mile loop that takes you through a landscape of boulders, rock formations, and the infamous Joshua trees.

THE INTEGRATRON: A fusion of art, science, and magic, this historical structure sits atop a powerful geomagnetic vortex in the magical Mojave Desert. It's located 20 miles north of the park and is constructed entirely of wood in the shape of a dome. Created by George Van Tassel, this energy vessel is believed to be an electrostatic generator for rejuvenation and time travel. Immerse yourself in a sound bath inside the dome where crystal singing bowls are played. The energy is unreal as the vibrations swirl around the structure, hitting your chakras and filling your senses with peace, relaxation, and a heightened sense of self.

NOAH PURIFOY OUTDOOR DESERT ART MUSEUM: Go on a walking tour of the Noah Purifoy Outdoor Desert Art Museum to take in Purifoy's incredible large-scale sculptures. This Joshua Tree outdoor museum is filled with installations that were created out of discarded materials, each telling a story and taking the viewer into the mind and experience of the creator.

PLACES TO STAY

THE JOSHUA TREE HOUSE, CASITA, AND HACIENDA: These are gorgeously curated Airbnbs with a strong attention to detail, ensuring that you feel connected to the desert and rested and relaxed. These stunning properties were created and designed by Sara and Rich Combs, who live in Joshua Tree full-time. The two have truly manifested a desert oasis that makes you never want to leave.

ROCK BOUND OASIS RETREAT: A beautiful midcentury modern desert house and casita built in 1954, this place is ideal for larger groups. Nestled up against some of the most breathtaking rock formations I've seen, it makes you feel as if you've got a slice of the park to yourself. The pool is perfect for escaping the summer heat, and in winter there is an epic bathtub that looks out into a cactus garden.

THE SHACK ATTACK: Removed from the hustle and bustle of the town, the Shack Attack is perfect for some quiet time. Expect endless views of the desert and beautifully curated decor that focuses on the outdoors and simplicity. Creators Kathrin and Brian Smirke have three projects in Joshua Tree that they have gutted and renovated themselves. Their other properties in Joshua Tree are Dome in the Desert and Cabin Cabin Cabin.

Utah and Arizona

DON'T MISS

ARCHES NATIONAL PARK: This park is located in Utah with more than two thousand natural sandstone arches. There is also a large array of hikes within this park, but the one I recommend the most is the quick 3-mile round-trip hike to the gigantic 60-foot freestanding sandstone Delicate Arch perched on a bowl-like cutout of a rock face. Be sure to go early to avoid tourists.

BRYCE CANYON NATIONAL PARK: This is an immense valley filled with spire-shaped rock formations called hoodoos. While it is easy to just drive up and admire the view, I highly recommend hiking into it to feel the energy of the hoodoos. Walking along the paths next to the giant natural sculptures truly makes you feel so tiny and in awe of Mother Nature.

MONUMENT VALLEY NAVAJO TRIBAL PARK: This place is unlike any landscape I have ever seen. Nestled near the Arizona-Utah border, the

towering bright red sandstone buttes instantly pull you in and make you feel so tiny and in awe of these natural wonders. Listening to the stories of the land, sensing the immense spiritual pull and the energy of lives before us, and seeing truly jaw-dropping views, you will keep this place with you forever. You can take a tour through the valley, or if you have a car that can handle some rough roads, you can venture in yourself, which I fully recommend. Each time I visit this place, it feels new and even more inspiring.

SLOT CANYONS: On Navajo land east of Page, Arizona, these canyons, of which there are many, are a labyrinth of curves and twists that play with the light as it cascades down onto the sandy floor. Water, flash floods, and wind have carved these canyons, leaving behind glorious sculptures that look like clay. The more frequently visited is Antelope Canyon, where you can hop on a guided tour, learning about every little curve and each storm that has dramatically changed the canyon. This landscape never seems to leave my mind—it just doesn't feel real—and I am constantly attempting to bring the beauty and colors of these canyons into my work.

ZION NATIONAL PARK: This is one of my favorite national parks to visit. The deep red cliffs tower overhead, forcing you to pause and be humbled by the greatness of the earth. There are a plethora of hikes to choose from, but if you are there on a short trip, a journey I never miss is the Narrows. This hike guides you up the Virgin River, where you actually trek through the water between the glorious canyons. Be sure to check the weather and be cautious of flash floods. Wear proper shoes and bring a hiking stick. For those who want a challenge, Angels Landing is stunning, but be advised that the 5-mile round-trip hike is strenuous—at times you are holding a chain bolted to the spine of the mountain. However, it grants you views of the entire valley that are more than worth the sweaty climb to the top.

PLACES TO STAY

AMANGIRI: Outside of Page, Arizona, Amangiri is a luxury resort that blends into the beautiful desert landscape, almost disappearing into the white-and-pink rock that surrounds the hotel. With stunning views from every room, the gorgeous setting offers a chance to really slow down, connect with your surroundings, and just be still. Views of the desert are framed by massive windows and cement cutouts that mimic the slot

canyons, letting in just the right amount of sunlight. This resort truly blurs the lines between indoor and outdoor, and its minimalist design honors functionality and beauty at the same time.

UNDER CANVAS ZION AND MOAB: These are glamping resorts. You get the feeling of camping but in beautiful tents that have real beds, nestled in stunning landscapes. I always make it a point to stay at an Under Canvas location. It feels like you are on an adventure with your friends, where you can have a drink, sip on a beer by the communal campfire, or retire to your room (some of which have a private tub and bathroom). This is camping elevated and it is one of the most fun experiences I have ever had while visiting the national parks.

THE VIEW HOTEL: This hotel has uninterrupted views of Monument Valley in each room. Waking up to the sun kissing the red desert sculptures takes your breath away. The hotel sits nestled into the landscape, almost disappearing into the rocks. If you can get a room on the third floor, the views at night are just as stunning as in the daytime. The stars seem to triple as your eyes adjust and the Milky Way appears. I have never seen so many stars in my life as I have in Monument Valley. Hiking into the valley is just feet from the hotel and driving through is just as easy. This is an ideal place to rest your head while visiting Monument Valley.

New Mexico

DON'T MISS

GHOST RANCH: This 21,000-acre ranch and retreat center is surrounded by the landscapes that Georgia O'Keeffe depicted so beautifully in her paintings time and time again. Here, you can take a tour of the actual landscapes she painted, visit her home and studio in Abiquiu, and fully immerse yourself in the world that O'Keeffe was so madly in love with. Visit for a day or plan a longer trip so you can stay.

SANTA FE: Known for its architecture and art, New Mexico's capital is buzzing with the creative arts, from jewelry to textiles, fine arts to pueblo architecture. This city never fails to inspire me. I have vivid memories of my first few visits—walking through the Georgia O'Keeffe Museum, talking with local artisans, and picturing myself living and creating there. I still hope someday to live at least part-time in Santa Fe, tucked away making art.

WHITE SANDS NATIONAL MONUMENT: Going to White Sands is like visiting another planet filled with white gypsum sand dunes as far as the eye can see. You can camp, hike, or day-trip. It is well worth venturing to southern New Mexico as there is truly no place like it. The stillness at sunrise or sunset truly is an unforgettable experience.

PLACES TO STAY

EL REY COURT: This is an eighty-six-room newly remodeled roadside inn in Santa Fe. Its tag line, "Where fast lives slow down," rings true. With perfectly curated design and beautiful minimalistic artwork gracing the walls, this spot has it all. The bar, La Reina, is perfect for cocktail hour or late-night hangs.

OJO CALIENTE: A stunning spa and resort near Taos, New Mexico, Ojo Caliente is known for its mineral hot springs. Disconnect, heal, and relax in this serene place where you can soak, hike, and connect with the stunning northern New Mexico landscape.

CHAPTER THREE

THE BEAUTY OF WORKING WITH YOUR HANDS

Working with your hands is such an honor. There's nothing that compares to the joy you feel when you've made something from scratch. When all is said and done and I stand back and look at what I've created, I feel a sense of accomplishment and peace. The culmination is truly one of my favorite parts of the process. And the true beauty of a handmade product is that it's never perfect. This quality of imperfection is what drew me to working with wood, an organic material that takes time to learn and care for.

Working through the imperfections in my chosen medium has taught me the importance of being present and giving the space and time to trudge through the tough spells. While growing, shifting, and evolving is important, it's also important to respect the original form and not alter its natural beauty too much—whether we're talking about wood or ourselves. This may sound a bit woo-woo, but as I've continued working with wood, it's become almost impossible to avoid drawing a parallel between my own inner growth and the growth of my craft.

When I'm creating, I focus not only on maintaining but also on highlighting the unique nuances in the wood in my hands. Grain plays a major role in my process, and I am continually seeking irregularities and beautiful blemishes. This process can be liberating, as there's no need to create a flawless product when working with wood.

I find that the most rewarding part of a project is sometimes the last step, conditioning the wood, when I get to smooth out all the rough edges and help a piece's natural beauty shine. There are various ways to treat and finish wood, and for me, it's important that I know exactly what goes onto and into the wood, especially when it's going to be in my home or used to serve food.

David Roost, founder of Roostmade Co., is a passionate, lifelong woodworker and friend of mine. Dissatisfied with the limited natural options for finishing wood, he developed a plant-based natural wood finish that comes in the form of an organic wood wax and an organic wood oil and is used to hydrate and protect cutting boards, butcher blocks, utensils, and other wood products. For every Roostmade product sold, three trees are planted to fight deforestation, and David has been generous enough to share a special Desert Soul Organic Wood Butter recipe for this book.

DESERT SOUL ORGANIC WOOD BUTTER BY DAVID ROOST, ROOSTMADE CO.

DIFFICULTY LEVEL: BEGINNER

Inspired by the healing spiritual vibes of the desert, this recipe was designed not only to protect and nourish your wood products but also to soothe your soul. The three essential oils used—palo santo, frankincense, and eucalyptus—all have antiseptic, antibacterial, and antimicrobial properties in addition to relaxing and spiritual benefits. Palo santo oil aids in mystical healing and has long been used by shamans to cleanse negative energy. Frankincense produces a heightened nourishing spiritual awareness. Eucalyptus oil is a positive, energy-lifting powerhouse. Pine resin has long been sacred to Native Americans for its healing and protective properties and it is commonly used in healing ceremonies to invoke clairvoyance, compassion, and spiritual strength. Organic beeswax is incorporated to nourish and protect the wood and it has a lovely naturally sweet scent to boot.

The primary carrier ingredient in this recipe is pure cold-pressed organic walnut oil, prized by Renaissance painters for its clarity and highly regarded by the finest woodworkers of modern day as well. This oil does not yellow over time, does not go rancid, and it naturally cures to turn into a semihard surface, offering excellent natural protection against the elements.

Those with severe allergies to walnut can use organic flaxseed oil as a substitute.

MAKES 8 FLUID OUNCES

INGREDIENTS

7 ounces organic walnut oil

.5 ounces organic yellow
beeswax

.5 ounces organic piñon
pine resin

30 drops palo santo
essential oil

15 drops frankincense
essential oil

15 drops eucalyptus
essential oil

To melt the oils and wax gently without burning the ingredients, make a simple double boiler on the stovetop: Pour 3 cups water in a small pot and place an 8-cup glass mixing bowl on top. Bring the water to a boil. (Do not cook in a pot directly on a heating surface—you must use a double boiler method or risk catching the oil on fire by overheating.)

Add the oil, beeswax, and pine resin to the bowl on top of your double boiler. Allow the steam from the boiling water to slowly melt and blend together all the ingredients, about 45 minutes. Stir frequently. There must be 1 to 2 inches of water in the pot at all times to create sufficient steam to melt the ingredients.

Remove the bowl from the double boiler. Allow the mixture to cool to about 120°F, about 20 minutes.

Add your essential oils to the bowl and mix thoroughly. Pour the mixture into an airtight glass container to cool completely. We recommend choosing a container with a wide mouth, as your wood butter once at room temperature will have a thick, honey-like consistency.

USAGE

This wood butter is a perfect all-natural wood conditioner for products that do not come into direct contact with food. The three essential oils in it are not consumable, so for conditioning items like cutting boards and coasters, please use a different food-grade wood conditioner. While protecting and moisturizing the wood, this product's lightweight finish leaves a smooth but natural feeling.

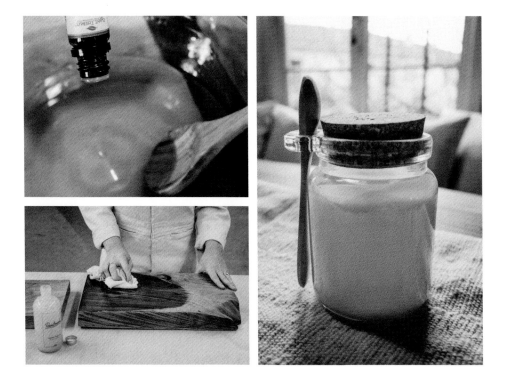

Because this finish is nontoxic, you don't need to worry if it gets on your hands—simply rub it in and enjoy the nourishing properties of these natural soothing ingredients!

Without regular oiling, cutting boards will absorb water and stains, dry out, crack, and split over time. Most wood-conditioning products out there consist of just mineral oil, a by-product of crude oil refining, which is not natural, has a high carbon footprint, and never fully cures. That's why I love this wood butter as an all-natural option.

To use, apply liberally on bare, clean, smooth wood. Use a cotton rag or your bare hands to work the butter deep into the pores of the wood, and rub, rub, rub. Allow the butter to penetrate the wood for 30 minutes and then buff vigorously with a clean cotton cloth until silky smooth. Then repeat, as two coats are recommended.

PRO TIP: *Use fine-grade steel wool to polish your wood surface after buffing for an extremely smooth finish. This process can be done anytime wood surfaces look dry.*

BECOMING CENTERED, STAYING IN THE PRESENT

While I love creating and then standing back to see what I've built, my absolute favorite part of what I do is something you can't see at all. What I love about my craft is that it requires me to remain present and centered at all times. To get to this place, so that my hands and my mind can connect and create, I need to find stillness. I discovered meditation through woodworking. It makes sense, given that my work revolves around repetitive motions, becoming present, and letting the flow happen. I often lose myself while I'm creating, and my work takes me outside of myself, to a different realm.

Let's take a moment to open up and to prepare for an inner creative journey with this exercise for tuning in, self-affirmation, and intention setting.

INTENTION SETTING MEDITATION WITH TANYA JONES

Tanya Jones is a holistic healer and teacher who has guided me through times of beauty and darkness in my own life. She created the following meditation specifically for this book. It is one that can help you to define your creative intention and it is meant to be revisited whenever you feel stuck creatively.

To Begin

Get into a comfortable position, seated upright in a chair with your hands resting on your lap, or sit on the ground cross-legged with your index finger and thumb touching on both hands.

Cleansing Breath

Close your eyes and take three cleansing breaths, inhaling in through your nose and exhaling out through your mouth. Make your inhales deep and your exhales audible, sighing with an "ahhhh" to intensify the cleansing quality of the breath. As you inhale, imagine light flowing in like an ocean wave; as you exhale, focus on removing negativity and clearing your body for meditation. Let it go and then let it flow, transitioning to a slow natural breath after your third cycle.

Grounding Breath

Do a body scan three times: Breathe in through your feet, all the way up to the crown of your head and then exhale down from the crown and out through your feet. Connect to your breath and the sensations of the body. As you inhale, imagine that the earth's energy is rising up inside of you like a mountain. As you exhale, imagine your energy

pushing into the earth like roots. Feel the stability of this connection grounding you.

Mantra

Raise your hands in a prayer position to your heart. Take a moment to give yourself some love, feeling the warmth from your hands penetrating your chest. Begin to mentally vibrate: "I" as you inhale and "am" as you exhale. Continue this breath, adding a personal mantra or intention to this phrase: "I" as you inhale and "am . . . present" as you exhale. "I am . . . accomplishing my goals." "I am . . . freedom." Whatever your intention, continue breathing it into that heart space. Feel it, see it, and tune into the emotion as if it were already so.

Celestial Helper

When you are ready, imagine a beautiful celestial helper appearing before you holding a large silver vessel. Release your hands from your heart and allow your intention to pour out of you like a sunbeam filling the vessel. Continue to mentally vibrate your mantra, breathing in "I," exhaling "am . . ." As you radiate your intention toward the vessel, see it turn from silver to gold. When the vessel has become completely gold, see your helper raise it up to the sky and then pour it into your body at the crown of your head. Feel the sensation of cosmic energy raining down inside of you like the Milky Way, dropping seeds of your intention into the fertile earth below. Continue to breathe, allowing the vision to evolve as seeds sprout and a garden rises up around you. Bask in this creation. Let it speak to you and inspire you.

Closing Meditation

When you are ready to close the meditation, imagine picking a flower from your garden and giving it to your celestial helper. Thank them for their assistance.

Bring your hands back to your heart.

Breathe in "I" and exhale "am . . ."

Slowly open your eyes.

Breathe in "I" and exhale "am . . ."

Raise your arms up above your head, inhaling "I," and stretch them out to circle your body with a last cleansing exhale: "Ahhhh."

Take your time with each section of the meditation. If you would like to increase the cleansing breath to five cycles, and the grounding breath to ten, absolutely do so.

SOME NOTES BEFORE YOU GET STARTED
ON THE MEDITATION . . .

MAKE A RITUAL SETTING FOR MEDITATION: Create a sacred space for your meditation. Burn sage, light candles, and set crystals around you.

SET A TIMER: If you have a time constraint, you may want to set a timer. This will alert you when you need to say goodbye to your celestial helper and close the meditation.

TAKE A CLEANSING BREATH: Practicing this breath helps release any energy of the day that might interfere with you being present for meditation. Extend your cleansing breath to additional cycles if you are having a particularly rough day!

TAKE A GROUNDING BREATH: This breath helps you to become present and grounded while acting as a bridge to your physical and spiritual bodies. This is crucial for entering the meditative state. Extend the breath to additional cycles if you wish.

WORK WITH A MANTRA: The "I am . . ." mantra will assist you in the embodiment of your intention. It is best not to have too many intentions. I encourage limiting it to one to three per meditation, allowing you to stay focused as much as possible. Placing your hand on your heart is a gesture of love and emotion—dive in and feel it. This will fuel your intention and give it the velocity to speak with the infinite. Once you begin the mantra portion of the meditation, you will continue it through the end.

INCORPORATE SCENT: Burn sage or palo santo for added aromatherapy. Burning these scents cleanses the energy of the space and clears the mind.

HYDRATE: Drink lemon water.

WABI-SABI: BRINGING THE BEAUTIFUL
AND THE IMPERFECT INTO YOUR HOME

My home is where I want to feel inspired, and it's important for me to start my day with calming energy. I have designed my living space to be a sanctuary, a reflection of a soothing state that helps manifest my well-being. In my life and in my woodworking, I follow the Japanese practice of wabi-sabi, an approach to design and life that dates back to the twelfth century. Wabi-sabi teaches us that there is beauty to be found in the simple, the messy, the natural, the impermanent, and the imperfect. So much of life seems to be about constantly seeking perfection. But by incorporating imperfections at home and in our creative process, we can reset our way of thinking. By bringing wabi-sabi into my life, my home, and my studio, I am shifting my perspective and celebrating imperfection.

DECLUTTER YOUR SPACE

Wabi-sabi is about a life of mindfulness and acceptance. We truly don't need much to get by, let alone to be happy, and none of it has to be flawless. In fact, we can find beauty in every blemish.

Take a look around your space and take stock of what you have. Are you holding on to unnecessary things? Spend some time clearing space in all the areas of your home: kitchen, living room, bedroom, bathroom, and your closet. Get rid of any items that are no longer serving you. I try to keep only items that have a function, that are purely decorative, or that are extremely sentimental. Push yourself—if you don't need an item, it's time to let go. A good rule of thumb is that if you haven't used or touched something for a year, you should part ways. Getting rid of these unused items opens you up for a life of intention and forces you to become present in the way you live. It removes distractions and lets you truly focus on what is meaningful. Negative space is just as important as the space an object itself occupies. Let the special items you decide to keep have room to breathe.

IDENTIFY A COLOR SCHEME

Go back to your journaling exercise in chapter 2. What hues did you gravitate toward? I prefer to keep it simple and select one or two

colors, using different shades of them throughout my space. A base of neutrals and watered-down versions of your favorite hue is a great place to start. Anyone who knows me knows I love my neutrals (bring on the beige jokes), mostly earth tones and white. I meld a spectrum of these into my space to exude a sense of unity and calm, while also maintaining a sense of direction. This is an example of the way that I pull natural elements that inspire me into my space. From the colors of the sand meeting the frothy white waves to the burnt orange of high-desert rock formations to the calm neutrals of a hot desert day, I draw from landscapes that move me. Consider where you go in your mind, and where you go physically, that brings you peace. Bring that into your home.

BRING TEXTURE INTO YOUR SPACE

Texture adds depth and character to any space without creating clutter. I love incorporating unifying materials that feel good and add to the comfort of my home. I seek out materials that are sturdy, easy to clean, versatile, and easily and locally sourced if possible. I'm all about goods that are created nearby, particularly by my crafty friends. For this exercise, I have broken down all the materials in my home by color and function.

NEUTRAL, WHITE, AND OFF-WHITE
Textiles

Textiles play a huge role in my home. From curtains to table runners, to wall hangings, to sheets, textiles made of linen, wool, and cotton are my simple go-tos that can be changed out with the seasons and cared for easily. Linen, a favorite of mine, is beautiful but also practical. In the summer, an off-white linen sheet set keeps us cozy

in bed without getting too hot. To let in a natural flow of light, open-weave linen curtains frame my windows. The beauty of linen is that the texture differs with every piece, and it comes in so many shades and weaves, all of which only get better with use. Keep in mind that choosing linen in a brighter shade of white keeps a space feeling fresh and airy.

Cotton is soft, durable, and practical, and it can take a beating. It's ideal for place mats and durable dish and bath towels, all of which can be easily tossed in the wash as needed. In the winter, I swap out our linen bedding with a heavier cotton for extra warmth.

Wool is a wintertime go-to. When it starts to cool down, I break out the assortment of wool blankets that I've been collecting since college. Needless to say, I am very selective with each one that makes its way into my home. I usually go with a vintage Pendleton or army blanket for the base of my bed and for the couch.

I also love hanging blankets and tapestries on the wall as art. It brings a sense of softness and movement to the walls and offers a different spin on showing off the beautiful fabrics you have collected. One of my favorite works of art in my home is a handmade blanket tapestry, which creates the perfect backdrop to my dining area, by SoCal-based artist Küdd:Krig. She makes pieces with such care that her blankets can hang on the wall as art or be used for snuggling into on the couch.

Because off-white and white rugs are hard to keep clean, I've purposely selected materials that are natural and incredibly durable and that can take a beating and age well with wear. Jute is an excellent example of durable but simple material that can add texture to your space. A sheepskin rug placed on top of seating or at the foot of the bed adds a layer of texture to the furniture as well as a cozy place to sit or rest your feet after getting out of bed.

- Washed linen bed sets that are durable and so soft: Parachute Home
- Linen curtains: Restoration Hardware
- Throw blankets: Jungmaven
- Wool blankets: Pendleton
- Blanket tapestries: Küdd:Krig Home
- Sheepskin rugs: Shepherdess

Ceramics

Functional and beautiful, ceramics are a great choice to keep on display. I have a collection in a range of neutral colors and textures that I use daily. SVEN Ceramics, run by creative partners Sven and Mallie, is one of my favorite ceramics studios in San Francisco. I love the handmade perfections and imperfections of their work, knowing that each piece was thoughtfully created. Also in San Francisco is ceramicist Sam Lee, whose work, from her light fixtures to her vases, mugs, and bowls, will always have a place in my home.

BROWN, BEIGE, AND TAUPE

Furniture

This is probably no surprise, but I love all kinds of wood furniture, whether ash or walnut or redwood. Incorporating different types of woods in various pieces of furniture—coffee table, lamps, dining table, benches—helps warm up my space. I love mixing up the colors of my cutting boards as well. Mismatched boards in walnut and ash create a look that's loose and that doesn't take itself too seriously. As an artist, I'm naturally drawn to supporting other creators, and thus my home is filled with goods from local makers. It makes every piece special while also inspiring me and reminding me of the hustle to keep

creating. These are my most cherished pieces in my home, like the dining table that my dear friend Katie and I made together and the credenza by Four / Quarter that holds our massive record collection.

I also gravitate toward leather. It only looks better with age and is easy to clean, and if it gets scratched, no worries, that's an easy fix, too. Leather warms up a space and is a no-fuss material that is inviting to sit on. I was on the hunt for a timeless leather couch that my fiancé and I could both easily stretch out on and found a beautiful one from CB2 that's breaking in perfectly. I also added in a daybed that doubles as a bench for the dining table. From couches to chairs, to my wallet and my shoes, I turn to leather for its durability. It looks better the more I use it, making it worth the investment. At the same time, my favorite leather-and-wood sling-back chair is from Saffron + Poe, and no one is allowed to sit in it because it's so damn pretty. I also have two Saffron + Poe chairs in my shop. The two at the shop are woven leather and keep looking better with wear.

Another creative solution using warm tones and wood is open shelving in the kitchen, perfect for showing off my collection of ceramics. A simple floating shelf or open cabinet offers an opportunity to display a curated set of your favorite possessions. Arrangement, too, makes a big difference. Functional pieces like couches, chairs, and tables should guide you through the space. When planning the design of your home, think about how you would like your guests to experience your space when you're entertaining.

WHERE TO SOURCE
- Custom furniture: Katie Gong and Four / Quarter
- Wood and leather chairs: Saffron + Poe
- Leather couches: CB2
- Cutting boards: Shop on the Mesa
- Wooden lamps: Lostine

GREEN

Plants

Houseplants are the perfect way to bring the inspiration of nature into your home. Not only do plants have a calming effect, but they literally clean the air in your space. Aesthetically, I tend to like to make a statement with my greenery. Selecting one to four large plants creates a focal point—I have a huge bird-of-paradise, a fiddle leaf fig, and two large cacti. They all require different care so placement and regular attention is very important. Taking care of my plants also creates a daily ritual for me that celebrates being present and caring for something outside of myself. The plants in my home all entered my life at different times and are a part of my history.

WHERE TO SOURCE
- Indoor and outdoor plants: Flora Grubb Gardens
- Cacti: Half Moon Bay Nursery
- Budget plants: local hardware stores

SMALL POPS OF COLOR

Art, Rugs, and Mirrors

New art is continually filtering into my home. Often I see a piece and know that I can't live without it, and it becomes a fresh point of inspiration. I will always be a collector for so many reasons, one being that I am constantly seeking creative stimulus. It's a way to spark conversation, a new perspective, and the drive to create. Art can serve as a statement piece or tie a room together. Naturally, some of my most loved pieces are from friends. The works of Meryl Pataky, a neon artist out of Oakland, are a favorite of mine. Not only is her work visually compelling, but it also communicates a narrative that she is urging the viewer to take part in. My dear friend Katie Gong creates

abstract wooden sculptures in which she bends and ties wood into knots. These pieces act as table sculptures, hanging pieces, and wall-mounted work. Her artwork brings a sense of calm into any space. Heather Day, out of San Francisco, creates abstract paintings that make for beautiful statement pieces. She creates splashes of color that play with minimalism and reflect how things feel rather than how they look. Carrie Crawford, of Mineral Workshop, makes beautifully dyed fabrics that transform shapes into organic gestures and are then stretched, framed, and hung on the wall. Jimmy Brower of West Perro in Oakland builds beautiful wall hangings that are inspired by the desert landscape and the beauty of traveling.

When I decorate a space, I start with the groundwork. Rugs build a palette for furniture while also adding stylish flair to a space. I love playing with layers, placing rugs with pattern and color over a neutral base. One of my favorite pairings is a subtle jute rug with a thick weave, topped with a bright shag rug for a pop of color and extra texture. Taib Lotfi and Kenya Knight's rug shop, Soukie Modern, in Palm Springs has a beautiful collection of Moroccan rugs from Lotfi's hometown. For large-area jute rugs, World Market is a great resource.

In art and life, I am forever chasing the light. A trick I've learned for small spaces is to place a mirror across from a window. It'll open up the space, reflect the light, and give the illusion of another window. I am drawn to dramatic floor-length mirrors and circular mirrors. A large floor mirror is not only functional, but it's also a simple design element that can tie together a room while reflecting the outdoors and the colors in your home.

CREATING A FEELING IN YOUR SPACE

SCENT: I love the smell of palo santo. I burn it every day in my home, keeping small bowls in every room with a few sticks in them that I can frequently light.

LIGHTING: It's all about setting the mood. I like warm, low lighting in my space. I like to bring in a gilded look with lots of Edison bulbs. I ditch any bulbs that have a green or blue hue and use the same color bulbs throughout my home. The wattage of your lamps should be bright enough to shine a light on your task but not so bring that it hurts to look at.

SIMPLICITY: Your space is just like you, perfectly imperfect, so don't sweat the small stuff. Use a few of the objects you have gathered in your journey so far—your inspirations, your colors, your textures. And keep it simple.

CALM: Last but not least, set up a space in your home for meditation. Maybe it's a pile of pillows by the window, a cozy corner of the couch, or a comfy daybed, but make sure that it serves as a little sanctuary where you find rest and can reset and center yourself.

Creating a space that is your own is so rewarding. When opening the door to your home, you should feel like you are entering a place of safety, rest, and freedom—to create, to make a mess, to sit and be calm, and to be yourself.

DAYBED (16 x 27 x 74 INCHES)

One of my favorite spots in my home is my daybed. I use it as seating for my dining-room table, as a spot for lounging and meditating, and as a place for guests to sleep. It is versatile and adds charm to my space while keeping it clean and modern. Here is how I created mine.

SUPPLIES

Two ¾-inch x 4-foot x 8-foot pieces of sanded plywood

Measuring tape

Pencil

Wood glue

1¼-inch 18-gauge brad nails

Deckmate 1¼-inch star flat-head wood deck screws

Deckmate 3-inch star flat-head wood deck screws

60-grit sandpaper for an orbital sander

Optional: Polycrylic wood finish, paint-rolling tray, and small foam paint roller

Urban Outfitters 74 x 27 x 6-inch Rohini Daybed Cushion

Safety glasses

Respirator

Gloves

TOOLS

Circular saw guide

Nine 6-inch clamps

Circular saw

18-gauge brad nail gun

Drill with star bit

Orbital sander

STEP ONE: MAKE THE BENCHTOP

For this particular design, we will be using plywood to construct the entire bench, giving it a seamless, minimalistic feel. We'll start by measuring the benchtop panel, which will comprise three separate panels glued and nailed together. Each panel will measure 27 x 74 inches to accommodate the cushion.

Lay one 4 × 8-foot sheet of plywood on the worktable. Measure and mark 27 inches from the width end. Repeat for the other end.

Place your circular saw guide down and clamp it on both ends. A circular saw has a foot (base of the saw) where the blade comes out. In order to cut right on your line, you must account for the base of the saw and the saw itself, usually 1¼ or 1½ inches. You will place the saw guide 1¼ inches away from the center line so that when you run your saw down the plywood you will be cutting right on the line. So, to cut a 16-inch piece, measure at 14¾ inches (if the base track is 1¼ inches wide) to get the blade on the 16-inch mark. Make the cuts. Repeat two times.

For each of the three panels, measure and mark 74 inches from the length end and make the cuts. You should now have three 27 × 74-inch panels.

STEP TWO: CUT THE BENCH LEGS

Now that you've got the benchtop ready to go, the next step is cutting the legs. Each of the 3 legs will comprise 3 panels nailed together. You'll be making 9 panels total.

Lay the second 4 × 8-foot sheet of plywood on the worktable. Measure, mark, and cut two 16 × 96-inch panels to match the width of the top.

Cut down the height of the legs so that the legs are 13¾ inches tall to create a total bench height (with top) of 16 inches (22 inches with the cushion). Gradually the cushion will compress over time, creating a bench height of about 20 inches, which is ideal for sitting!

Once you have cut down all 9 panels, you are ready to attach them together.

STEP THREE: ASSEMBLE THE BENCH LEGS

Take one leg panel, and generously apply wood glue to one side. Place the next panel on top. Using your nail gun, nail them together around the border, adding a few nails in the center just for security. You don't need to overdo it with the nails—4 per side of each leg should do it.

Glue the opposite side of the first panel, press a third panel on top, and then nail that from the other side so that all 3 panels are securely glued and nailed together.

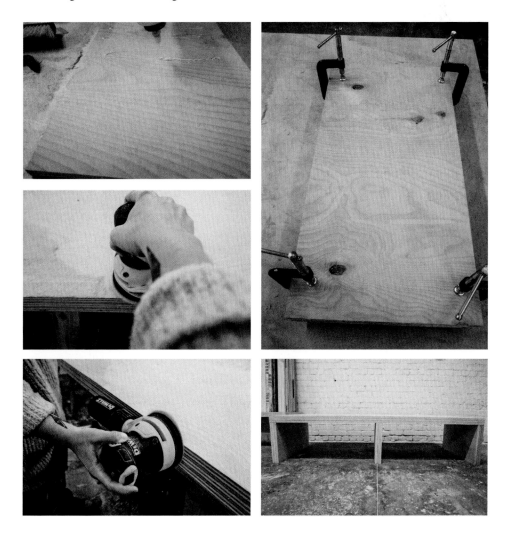

Using four 1¼-inch deck screws, drill the legs together from one side to ensure that the legs stay tight. Use 3 screws evenly spaced on each leg. Repeat for all 3 bench legs.

STEP FOUR: ASSEMBLE THE BENCHTOP

This process is identical to what you did for the legs. Lay one plywood panel down and apply wood glue to its surface. Place the second panel on top, making sure all the edges are as flush as possible. Don't worry if it's not perfect—you can always sand the edges to get it there if necessary.

Use the nail gun to nail the panels together. Use as many nails as you need to reduce any gaps between the layers.

Apply wood glue and lay the third panel on top, securing it with brad nails in the same fashion.

Drill together the 3 panels with the 1¼-inch deck screws—2 in each corner, 3 at the center, 4 in between on the sides (19 total).

STEP FIVE: ATTACH THE LEGS TO THE TOP

Now that your bench legs and benchtop are glued and affixed, you can put it all together! Line up the first leg with one side of the benchtop, making sure it sits flush underneath the edge as well as with the front and back of the top. Drill a pilot hole in the corners and middle edge to ensure the screws will sink in nicely and not split the plywood.

Once you have your pilot holes drilled, drive three 3-inch deck screws into the leg from the top of your bench. Make sure they hit the center of your leg to avoid any screws shooting out the sides.

Apply the same method to the opposite side, making sure everything is flush and even. After your exterior legs are in place, slide in the middle leg and drill your pilot holes and screws to secure the leg in place. Almost done!

STEP SIX: FINISH THE BENCH

Walk around the bench, looking for flaws in the alignment between the legs and top. (It is unlikely to be perfect.)

Attach the sandpaper to the orbital sander. Hold down the wood with one hand while you sand with the other, smoothing out any differences between the 3 plywood panels.

Optional: For a more finished feel, pour wood finish into the paint-rolling tray and apply it to the bench with the paint roller. One coat will do. Personally, I prefer the more natural look of plywood.

Now you're ready to throw that cushion on there and enjoy!

SAFETY TIPS

Ask a friend for help when lifting heavy lumber and plywood.
Make sure you are comfortable using a drill, circular saw, and sander.
If you have long hair, tie it back.
Always wear the proper safety glasses and respirator.
Keep fingers away from the saw blade, drill bit, and sander.

CHAPTER FOUR

COMMUNITY OVER COMPETITION

I have so much to say on the subject of being a woman in a traditionally male-dominated industry. Where to begin? This is a subject that has both plagued me and pushed me to be better through the years, with countless lessons that I've learned along the way. When I first started out, my ego was tender and delicate. The tough criticism I would receive, mostly from men, really struck a nerve. Criticism came in the form of online comments, emails, and a few in-person remarks at trade shows. I'd hear things like "Women should never operate power tools" and "Her daddy must have paid someone to make that for her because there is no way she did it herself." I took these comments personally and often found myself in tears as I searched for a way to defend myself and show these people who I really was. I had so many doubts and insecurities about my abilities. Would I ever be good enough to match up to my male peers? How much of my femininity did I need to suppress to earn respect in my field? While I was busy seeking answers and trying to change myself to suit the industry, the truth revealed itself: The questions themselves needed to be questioned.

Initially, my default was always to assume that the cards were stacked against me. As a fiercely independent woman, I have an ego that would tell me that asking for help would mean that I was weak. I was determined to do it all on my own. I would load up my car with lumber, cut massive pieces, and carry very heavy completed furniture to wherever I was headed. There were many close calls in which I could have seriously injured myself. Looking back, I wonder why I needed to prove that I could do it all alone. Did it make me stronger or grant me access into some inner boys' club? No, it did not. Did I need the acceptance of men to validate what I was doing? Um, that's a hard no.

Today, I no longer feel like I have to prove myself to anyone. My unique position as a woman in a male-dominated field is something that has made me stronger, and more aware of my femininity, and it's a power that can always be harnessed. I love talking to other incredible female makers in my community who challenge and inspire my point of view. Meryl Pataky, my dear friend who is a neon artist, is also immersed in a profession dominated by men. We talk constantly about our roles as females, as makers, and as aspiring masters of our craft. I asked Meryl what it's been like paving her own path in an industry dominated by men. Her answer: "In my experience, I've found that the masters in my trade (many of them men), despite their immense skill and pride, seem to be intimidated by assertive and talented women rising up and presenting their craft through a different lens.

Respect the masters, but never be bound by what they expect of you."

For years, I struggled with even using the term *woodworker*. I had been told by so many contractors and cabinetmakers that what I was doing wasn't woodworking but rather "wood art." I felt that I needed to earn the title of woodworker, and only recently have I felt comfortable embracing the term. It seems silly now. I work with wood, day in and day out, and there is absolutely no reason why I shouldn't use this term for what I do.

Doubt and insecurities plague all of us. We tell ourselves stories about who we are and what we are supposed to be, and it can be challenging to break free from these limiting narratives. For years, my woodworking environment was purely functional. The space I worked in was dirty with no frills, and I purchased lower end tools.

Then one day as I was feverishly working on fulfilling holiday orders, I looked around and thought, "This space needs some love." Why had I been working for so long in a space that didn't represent who I was? I realized I'd been telling myself that I didn't yet "deserve" an inspiring space because my woodworking skills were not yet up to some imaginary level that I had created for myself. But in that moment, I knew I had to make a huge change and abandon this way of thinking.

My business was growing, and I wanted my work space to be a place that reflected my creative vision. So I took on the task of completely redoing my shop, building new benches and storage units, upgrading all my tools, and painting the entire 1,000-square-foot space. And the cherry on top: I added a showroom. I needed my work space to feel like home, to fill me up with inspiration, and to be a place that I was proud of.

An inspiring work space is not something that needs to be earned. It's an essential piece of doing your best creative work. When I embarked on my studio revamp, I knew I was going to have to ask for help. My partner in life and my right-hand man at work, Antrom, helped me plan and build out the remodel. Having two sets of hands made all the difference, and it made me realize how far I'd come in being able to accept help. Together we created a new workbench and lumber storage wall for my space and showroom. Now it's your turn.

WORKTABLE

DIFFICULTY LEVEL: ADVANCED

SUPPLIES

3 Burro Brand 24-inch sawhorses

Two 4 x 8-foot sheets of birch plywood

Measuring tape

Pencil

Deckmate 2-inch star flat-head wood deck screws

Four 2-inch x 4-inch x 8-foot pieces of Douglas fir lumber

Deckmate 3-inch star flat-head wood deck screws

Optional: Polycrylic wood finish, paint-rolling tray, and small foam paint roller
Safety glasses

TOOLS

Drill with star bit

Miter saw

STEP ONE: LINE UP THE SAWHORSES TO MAKE THE BASE

In this project, you will be making a 4 × 8-foot worktable. If your space does not accommodate this size, have your lumberyard cut the plywood according to your needs.

Measure and mark your sheets of birch plywood into 3 equal sections. For this 4 × 8-foot table, place one sawhorse beneath the center of one sheet of plywood (48 inches from the length end) and the other 2 sawhorses at 24 inches from each length end, respectively.

STEP TWO: ATTACH THE BOTTOM PLYWOOD TO THE SAWHORSES

Now that your 3 sawhorses are lined up with the bottom sheet in place, drill four evenly spaced 2-inch deck screws through the plywood, making sure to hit the center of the sawhorse underneath. Repeat for each sawhorse. This makes the base of your worktable sturdy and secure.

STEP THREE: PREP AND INSTALL THE INTERIOR FRAME

With the birch plywood base fixed to your sawhorses, you can now line up the Douglas fir pieces to build the interior frame of the table. You will be building a frame around the edges of the base. Place one of the Douglas fir pieces along the outer long-side edge of the birch base, making sure it sits flush. If this beam is longer than the base, trace the overhang and cut off that excess portion with a miter saw. Make sure to properly secure the wood on the miter saw, keep your hands clear from the blade, and start the saw before making your cut. To make the cut, start the saw and pull down on the saw handle. Continue running the blade until you have fully cut the wood.

To secure this beam in place, drill 4 evenly spaced 3-inch deck screws through the bottom sheet of plywood and up into the beam. Make sure to center your screws into the beam. Repeat with a second piece of Douglas fir for the opposite side.

Measure the distance between the interior of the 2 beams that you just secured on your plywood to get your crossbeams. You'll want them to sit snugly inside each outer beam. First start with both ends, then add one beam at 48 inches (over your center sawhorse) for extra support. Using the 3-inch deck screws, secure each side beam to the crossbeam to fasten them all together. One screw from the outside beam into the center beams should suffice.

STEP FOUR: MOUNT YOUR TOP

With the beams now secured to the base, place your top sheet of birch plywood onto the beams, making sure all sides are as flush as possible. Using your drill, secure the top using the 3-inch deck screws—one in each corner and at the 48-inch center mark on both sides. Make sure the screws are flush or slightly recessed to avoid anything catching on the surface of your tabletop.

STEP FIVE: APPLY THE FINISH (OPTIONAL)

If you prefer to keep your birch au naturel, skip this step. However, if you want your tabletop to have more of a sheen, pour wood finish into the paint-rolling tray and apply it to the top of your table, which will help protect the birch from spills and wear. One coat will do.

All done! Now you can start building whatever your heart desires with your new worktable.

SAFETY TIPS

Ask a friend for help when lifting heavy lumber and plywood.
Make sure you are comfortable using both a drill and miter saw.
If you have long hair, tie it back.
Always wear the proper safety glasses.
Keep fingers away from the saw blade and drill bit.

LUMBER STORAGE WALL

DIFFICULTY LEVEL: ADVANCED

SUPPLIES

Four 4-inch x 4-inch x 8-foot pieces of Douglas fir lumber

Measuring tape

6-inch star deck screws

Ten 4 x 8-foot sheets of birch plywood

Deckmate 3-inch star flat-head wood deck screws

42 Simpson strong tie ZMAX 2 x 4-inch 12-gauge galvanized medium L-angle brackets

$\frac{5}{8}$-inch Phillips drive sheet metal screws

Safety glasses

TOOLS

Miter saw

Drill with star bit

Two 6-inch C-clamps

98-inch circular saw cutting guide

Circular saw

STEP ONE: MAKE THE BASE

Determine how much lumber you'll want to store and how much space you have to work with. This particular lumber storage system requires a rear wall, and the instructions here are based on an 8-foot wall. This project is most effectively carried out with the assistance of a second person, so grab a friend if you can!

Begin by building the skeleton (interior frame). Lay 2 Douglas fir pieces side by side. Make sure they are exactly the same length. They will most likely be slightly different, so use your miter saw to make any necessary adjustments. Make sure to properly secure the wood on the miter saw, keep your hands clear from the blade, and start the saw before making your cut. To make the cut, start the saw and pull down on the saw handle. Continue running the blade until you have fully cut the wood.

Place both pieces of wood on the ground so that the outer edge of each end measures 4 feet apart. Measure the distance between the inside of both pieces: That will be your center beam length.

Using your interior measurement as a template, cut 5 identical beams from your lumber—1 for each end and 3 that are evenly dispersed in the middle. You'll want to write down where you spaced them, as you'll be drilling your plywood into these sections. For an 8-foot base, placing each beam 2 feet apart keeps it simple and sturdy.

Drill 6-inch screws from the outside of the 4-inch × 4-inch × 8-foot fir pieces to secure the middle beam in place, one screw on each side of the 4 × 4 × 8s. Repeat for the opposite side until all pieces are secured together. Skeleton complete!

STEP TWO: ATTACH THE BOTTOM PLY TO THE INTERIOR FRAME

Now that your interior frame is complete, lay 1 birch plywood sheet on top and drill 3-inch deck screws every 6 to 8 inches to secure it down. Be sure to drill evenly into each corner and at the center of all the beams, keeping in mind where they are spaced underneath. This will ensure that the birch plywood will not budge.

STEP THREE: BUILD THE REAR AND SIDE WALLS

Now you'll build the side and rear walls. If you plan on storing plywood, you'll want at least one of these walls to be 4 feet wide. Line up a sheet of birch plywood with the back of the base. Make sure it is flush with one edge. Drill 6-inch screws through the bottom of the plywood (from the back) into the base to secure it in place. Four screws across should keep it in place while you are assembling the rest.

Repeat those steps for the other half of the base to complete the back wall. The 2 pieces of plywood will now be attached vertically to the base to give you an 8-foot-tall wall. Push the base into place and double-check this is where you want it to live.

Using the 3-inch deck screws, drill the plywood into studs of the existing wall in your studio to help keep them upright. Studs are usually spaced 16 or 24 inches apart. If you start in a corner and measure out 16 inches and you don't find a stud, you should find one at 24 inches. Drilling into studs will ensure that the plywood stays fastened to the wall of your space.

Once the rear is fastened, grab another sheet of plywood and place it on whichever side you'd like to use to store the larger lumber and plywood. This side will be the same width as the entire base.

Using 6-inch deck screws, secure the bottom of the plywood to the base, making it flush with the ground and the front of your base. Bind the plywood to the interior of your base and rear wall with L-angle brackets—2 brackets on the bottom into the base and 2 brackets on the rear wall should cover it.

STEP FOUR: MAKE THE LUMBER SEPARATORS

Now that your rear wall, plywood storage wall, and base are complete, you are ready to add the separating sheets of ply to help organize your lumber. This step depends heavily on your individual needs and what types of lumber you will be storing, but for the sake of this example, we'll go ahead and mimic what's in my space. And because you are just starting out, you'll want to keep the separators relatively simple and avoid complex angles.

The interior separating walls will be 3 feet deep and 6 feet tall. That way, there's enough support to hold everything together and ample space to store lumber. Lay 1 sheet of plywood on your worktable. Looking at the plywood horizontally, from one side measure 3 feet across and mark that with a pencil. To ensure cutting a straight line, we must measure to make the straight line. Measure 3 feet across from the same side at multiple points so that when you draw your line with a guide you will know you are on track. Line up the saw cutting guide so that you can track your circular saw at your mark. Clamp down the sides right on the marks you just made closest to the edge of the plywood. Trace the straight edge that is your line. A circular saw has a foot (base of the saw) where the blade comes out. In order to cut right on your line, you must account for the base of the saw and the saw itself, usually 1¼ or 1½ inches. You will place the

saw guide 1¼ inches away from the center line so that when you run
your saw down the plywood you will be cutting right on the line.

Use a C-clamp at each end to fix the guide to your plywood. Use the
circular saw to cut 12 inches from the plywood. Repeat the same
steps to reduce the height to 6 feet. Repeat those steps until you have
as many separating panels as you'd like. I recommend placing a panel
at 2 feet and another at 4 feet to store bigger lumber. Then place
4 more panels with each spread 1 foot apart for smaller lumber.

STEP FIVE: ATTACH THE LUMBER SEPARATORS
To attach the cut panels, have a buddy hold each panel while you use
your angle brackets to secure it in place (same process as your walls),

with 2 brackets attached to the base and 2 brackets drilled into the rear plywood panel. Make sure to use the 3-inch deck screws when drilling into the back wall. Most important, use only the ⅝-inch deck screws when drilling into the separator walls to ensure that nothing pokes through! Repeat these steps for each separator.

All done! You now have a very solid, practical, and aesthetically pleasing wall unit for storing your lumber.

SAFETY TIPS

Ask a friend for help when lifting heavy lumber and plywood.
Make sure you are comfortable using a miter saw, drill, and circular saw.
Always wear the proper safety glasses.
If you have long hair, tie it back.
Keep fingers away from the saw blades and drill bit.

CHAPTER FIVE

ALWAYS KEEP MAKING

I hope that by now you are feeling inspired and that your creative spark has been lit. This is where the real work begins, where the creative process becomes a practice, and the practice becomes a new way of life. At this juncture, I'd like to share one of my favorite mantras, which has guided me through many creative dry spells: *Always keep making*. When I am making, I am in a constant state of creative renewal, and cultivating this mind-set has allowed my art to become a way of life. There will be many times when things won't line up, when your materials will put up a fight, and when your vision for a project just won't pan out. At these times, it is more important than ever to keep this mantra in mind. Because if you can push through the frustration, you will learn the most about yourself and your work. These are the times when real change will happen.

"Always keep making" was at first just something that I aspired to—it wasn't always my process. There would be times when I would put my tools down in despair, thinking that it was time to give up. But after a break, I always somehow made it back to the studio. I listened to the voice in my head that told me to keep working through it, and I gave myself the gift of showing up.

It's impossible to exist in a constant creative high. It's not sustainable, just like living in a state of pure joy all the time is not sustainable. After all, we wouldn't appreciate moments of bliss without the dark, lost, scary times. The ups and downs are the most important times of creation. The moments just before inspiration strikes, when you pull yourself out of a rut to embark on a big project, are often the most fruitful. And they contain a kind of creative strength that can be stored and accessed again the next time around.

WOOD-FRAMED MIRROR

There will be times when you question your abilities, when your work might not feel up to par. That's where this mirror comes in. It can serve as a beautiful addition to your home, but it can also be a creative tool. Take a look into it when you need to remind yourself of the creative person you are.

SUPPLIES

1 sheet of ¾-inch pine plywood

1 IKEA Hovet mirror, measuring 30¾ x 77⅛ inches

Pencil

2 pieces of 1 x 10 x 80-inch or larger live-edge claro walnut

2 pieces of 1 x 4 x 80-inch walnut plus 4-inch x 2-foot scrap piece

Liquid Nails adhesive

Wood glue

1-inch finish nails

Shop rags

120-, 150-, 220-, 300-, and 400-grit sandpaper for an orbital sander

Gloves

Polycrylic wood finish

Safety glasses

Respirator

TOOLS

8-foot straight edge

Circular saw

Large clamps

Miter saw

18-gauge brad nail gun

Orbital sander

STEP ONE: CUT THE WOOD

Lay the plywood on a flat surface. Place the mirror on top of the plywood, with one corner of the mirror flush with one corner of the plywood (this will reduce the number of cuts you'll have to make). Using a pencil, trace the outline of the mirror onto the plywood. The plywood will be on the back of the mirror.

Remove the mirror from the plywood and set aside. Using the straight edge and clamps, cut off the excess plywood with the circular saw. A circular saw has a foot (base of the saw) where the blade comes out. In order to cut right on your line, you must account for the base of the saw and the saw itself, usually 1¼ or 1½ inches. You will place the saw guide 1¼ inches away from the center line so that when you run your saw down the plywood you will be cutting right on the line.

On your two live-edge walnut pieces, square up all edges that are not the live edge. Live edge is the natural side of the wood that has not been cut. It may still have a little bark on it and also a wavy line; that is, it will not have a manufactured straight cut side. Leave the live edge natural and funky while making all the other edges square and straight. The live edge will be on top of the mirror.

Using the miter saw cut all of your walnut pieces and your squared-off live-edge pieces to a length of 78⅝ inches.

Using the straight edge, clamps, and circular saw, cut your non-live-edge walnut pieces, which will be the sides of the mirror, to 3¼ inches wide. Those 2 pieces will be 78⅝ × 3¼ inches. From the scrap walnut, cut 4 pieces that are 4 × 3¼ inches. These will be the ends.

You are essentially building two ¾-inch boxes to cap the mirror on either side.

STEP TWO: ATTACH THE MIRROR TO PLYWOOD

Using the Liquid Nails adhesive, glue down the back edges of the mirror to the plywood. Let it sit to dry according to the manufacturer's specifications. Use clamps to hold in place.

STEP THREE: ASSEMBLE THE BOXES

Take your non-live-edge pieces—the sides—and line them up next to the long side of the mirror. There will be an overhang of 1½ inches. Split the difference so that ¾ inch hangs over on the top and the bottom. This piece will be on the outside of the mirror and plywood. Put adhesive on the edge of the mirror and wood glue on the edge of the plywood. Working from the bottom so that you hit the plywood and not the mirror, use the nail gun and finishing nails to secure the edge to the plywood. Take your time.

Take the 4 small 4 × 3¼-inch pieces and place them on the top and bottom of your two sides, with the 3¼-inch pieces matching the edges of your long pieces. Use wood glue and nails to secure these pieces into place. Wipe any excess glue with a rag.

Attach your live-edge pieces to the top sides of the mirror, matching all the edges and completing the boxes you made around the sides of your mirror. Use wood glue and nails to secure these pieces into place, being mindful to nail only wood to wood. Do not nail through the mirror! Work slowly. Wipe excess glue.

STEP FOUR: SAND THE WOOD

Attach the 120-grit sandpaper to the orbital sander. Sand down the walnut, smoothing out the imperfections. Repeat, using the 150-, 220-, 300-, and 400-grit sandpaper until the pieces are even and soft to the touch, with no rough edges.

STEP FIVE: FINISH THE WOOD

Put on your gloves and apply the wood finish with a clean rag, being careful not to get it on the mirror. Let the wood dry completely.

Bring the mirror home and admire your work!

SAFETY TIPS

Make sure you are comfortable using a circular saw, miter saw, brad nail gun, and sander.

Always wear the proper safety glasses.

If you have long hair, tie it back.

Keep fingers away from saw blade and sander.

While existing in a constant state of creation, it is also important to set goals for your projects. These goals can be simple, like spending a solo day at a museum to seek creative inspiration or setting a date by which you'd like to have a particular piece finished. Setting a concrete goal for a project opens up space for your creativity to flow freely, allowing that meditative flow state that I described earlier to set in as you are working.

As a culmination of the projects in this book, I want to send you off with what I consider the most challenging yet most rewarding of all: a dining table. Every time I build a dining table, the process holds such significance to me, because a dining table is such a meaningful object in a home. At my own table I've shared special meals and swapped stories with friends, I've sat in contemplative moments alone, and I've opened my heart to a loved one. A dining table is big and sturdy, and it hopefully lives on longer than we do, to be passed down from generation to generation, along with knowledge, stories, and love.

DINING TABLE AND BENCH BY KATIE GONG

DIFFICULTY LEVEL: MOST ADVANCED PROJECT OF THE BOOK!

I built the slab dining table and bench in my home with my dear friend Katie Gong, based on a design that she came up with. This is a more advanced project, so be sure that you are comfortable using all the tools involved before you get started.

We'll begin with an overview on creating slab furniture. Slab furniture is typically made from a thick cut of wood in which one o r multiple sides of the slab have been left natural and not squared off, meaning that the edges still have bark on them. Wooden slabs are naturally gorgeous and make for stunning and dramatic pieces of furniture.

DETERMINING THE SIZE

To decide on the size of your table, use masking tape to create a rectangle on the floor where the table will live. Make sure you leave adequate space between the table and your walls and other pieces of furniture. Typically, you want 16 to 24 inches of negative space around a table to accommodate chairs and/or benches. Think about how many people you'd like your table to seat—you need 20 to 24 inches per seat.

CHOOSING THE WOOD

Selecting a type of wood for your table can be a daunting task, as each type has its own nuances. Begin by doing an online search, and find some options that you are fascinated by, keeping in mind the other furniture you already have in your home and what will match well. I personally love claro walnut as it has the most grain patterns and a chocolaty color, and is hard so it holds up well over time. Locate a specialty hardwood shop in your area that sells wood slabs and plan a trip to peruse different types of wood. To save time, call first to ask whether the wood type you have in mind is available. In your research, pick out a few options that you like, as certain wood types may be more difficult to obtain.

BUYING THE WOOD

Once you find a slab that you like, double-check that your dealer is a trustworthy source and has treated all the wood for insects. Remember, you will be bringing this piece into your home. I recommend trying to buy Forest Stewardship Council (FSC)–approved wood, which ensures that your wood comes from a certified forest or postconsumer waste. The FSC sets standards on forest products. Eco-friendly woods are certified and labeled, and these labels identify products that come from well-managed forests that are sustainably farmed.

Remember that wood is priced by the board/foot, which is a fancy way of saying by volume. You'll be charged according to the length and width of a piece, as well as how thick it is. Most hardwood slabs are sold in a "quarter" system, referring to thickness. Wood milled to 4:4 is equivalent to 1 inch, 8:4 is 2 inches, 10:4 is 2.5 inches, and 12:4 is 3 inches. The thickness of a piece is completely up to you. Just note that the thicker the slab, the more expensive it will be, and the thinner the slab, the more support it will need. You'll also want to keep in mind thickness when considering how you'll surface your slab. Will you get it planed (a process of removing the uneven surface with a machine called a planer) or sanded? If you want to get your slab planed down, you should bump up its thickness first, as you'll lose a bit to surfacing. If you plan to do it yourself, sanding won't take off too much.

SURFACING

There are a few ways to surface your slab:

1. Locate a fabrication company that will plane your slab for you with a large planer or drum sander. This can be expensive, but it does save time.
2. Surface the slab top and the legs. This is a process of cleaning up the surface of the wood, sanding down imperfections, bark, and saw marks, and deep scratches so that it is even and smooth. Starting with 60-grit sandpaper, work your way up to 120-grit.

CUTTING DOWN YOUR PIECES

The woodworker's golden rule: Measure twice; cut once. Measure out all pieces, making sure that your saws will cut the thickness of the slabs that you have.

SANDING

Use an orbital sander. Start with 120-grit sandpaper (don't go lower as you'll add "chatter," aka scratches, to your top). Go with the grain. Use your hand to feel whether your surface is soft enough. Work your way up to 400 grit. Sand all your pieces.

GENERAL ASSEMBLY

Screw together all your table pieces (exact details on that below). Do a dry fit first. This practice run will ensure that all your cuts and measurements are correct and that everything fits together properly. Remember the golden rule: Measure twice; cut once. I like to use star bit screws for my main connections so that everything is super strong.

Start by screwing together the base. Then place the slab on top and screw that to the base. An extra set of hands is always helpful at this point. Make sure that the base is in the middle of the slab top. A good way to check your measurements and confirm you are centered is to make sure the measurement from the edge of your base to the edge of your table is the same on both sides. Repeat in the front and the back. Then screw together.

VARNISH

Find a varnish that you like and test it out on a small piece of your slab. Read the specifications of the varnish that you select and follow the manufacturer's instructions.

Now that we've gone over the general assembly instructions, we'll progress to the step-by-step assembly instructions for the top and base.

STEP BY STEP: HOW TO BUILD A 6-FOOT-LONG, 24-INCH-WIDE, 2-INCH-THICK REDWOOD SLAB TABLE

SUPPLIES

One 2 x 24 x 78-inch redwood slab for the top (buy a little more than you think to account for any trial and error)

One 2 x 24 x 36-inch redwood slab for the legs

One 2 x 8 x 78-inch piece of redwood for the spine

60-, 120-, 220-, and 400-grit sandpaper for an orbital sander

2-inch hex screws

3-inch hex screws

Varnish

Shop rag

Food-grade wood conditioner (optional)

Wood glue

Safety glasses

Respirator

Gloves

TOOLS

Draw knife, or chisel and hammer (optional; use only if you need to remove bark during step 2 surfacing)

Planer or drum sander (optional; use only if you're doing the step 2 surfacing work yourself)

Orbital sander

Drill with a hex drill bit

Circular saw

8-foot cutting guide (to cut the ends of your slabs)

Straight edge

CUT LIST

Redwood slab top:
2 x 24 x 72 inches

Two redwood slab legs:
2 x 24 x 28 inches each. The dimensions depend on the thickness of the slab top. The equation is total table height minus slab top thickness.

Redwood spine: 2 x 8 x 48 inches

STEP ONE: SELECT THE WOOD

Buy a slab for the top, a second slab for the legs, and a piece for the spine. They should be the same type of wood and ideally from the same tree. To keep a consistent look, I chose the same thickness for the slab top and the legs.

The spine will run underneath the top slab of the table and the bench, securing the legs to the table and providing structural integrity. You may be able to purchase at the finished width of 8 inches; if not, you can cut it yourself later. You'll be cutting down the length, so be sure to get enough when you purchase it to account for your saw and/or errors.

STEP TWO: SURFACE THE PIECES

Make sure the pieces are level. Again, unless you have access to a large planer or drum sander, I suggest you get this professionally done at the store where you are purchasing your pieces if this is an option. Most lumberyards and specialty hardwood shops will have slabs that are level and ready to go. That is where you will find the easiest selection of lumber for this project.

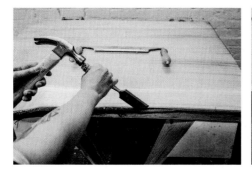 

Remove all excess bark with a draw knife if your slab still has bark on it. Hold on to the knife and pull toward you to shave off the bark. Use a chisel and a mallet for more stubborn pieces.

STEP THREE: SAND THE WOOD

Attach the 60-grit sandpaper to the orbital sander. Sand down the pieces, smoothing out the imperfections. Repeat, using the 120-grit sandpaper until the pieces are even and soft to the touch, with no rough edges.

STEP FOUR: CUT THE WOOD FOR THE TABLETOP

Using your saw of choice, cut and square up your slab top. Make sure your edges are straight. For this you can eyeball, but whatever straight line you make on one side, make sure the other end is parallel to it.

One trick for this is to measure from one corner to the opposite side and double-check the opposite corners are the same distance across. If they are, you know your edges are parallel.

STEP FIVE: CUT THE WOOD FOR THE LEGS

Cut the 2 leg pieces to height. Most dining tables are about 30 inches. Cut your legs to this height minus the thickness of the top. If the slab thickness is 2 inches, then cut your legs to 28 inches.

STEP SIX: CUT THE WOOD FOR THE SPINE

Cut the spine to 6 to 8 inches wide (if necessary) and the length of the table with the legs on. If your table is 6 feet long, then your bases

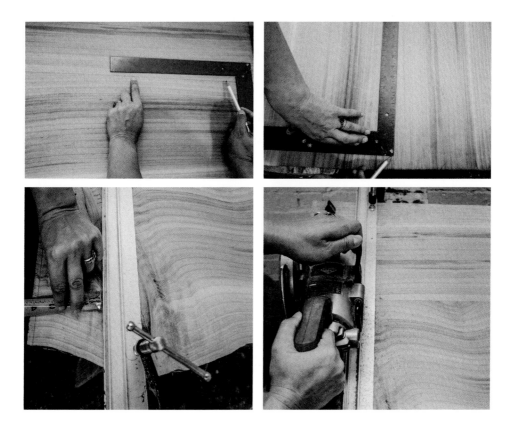

should be inset 1 foot on each end so someone can sit at either side. Make sure your spine is about 4 feet plus the thickness of your legs.

STEP SEVEN: DRILL HOLES IN THE SPINE

Drill 4 pilot holes evenly spaced along the center into the spine to avoid splitting the wood. This is where you'll attach your base to your slab top.

STEP EIGHT: SCREW THE LEGS INTO THE SPINE

With 2 slabs for legs, you can make 1 spine for the base. You will screw the 2 slab legs to the spine. To avoid splitting the wood, drill pilot holes. Drill 1 pilot hole in the top center of each spine leg 2 inches from the top. Screw the legs to the spine using the 3-inch hex screws.

STEP NINE: ATTACH THE BASE TO THE SLAB

Make sure that the screws you are using aren't too long or too short. You don't want to poke through the top, but you want it to be secure. For example, if your spine piece is 2 inches thick, then a 3-inch screw should cover it. Use the 3-inch screws to secure your spine to the base. Follow the pilot holes you made so that you do not split the wood.

STEP TEN: SAND THE WHOLE TABLE

Attach the 220-grit sandpaper to the orbital sander and sand the table again. Repeat, using the 400-grit sandpaper. Take your time while refining your slab and giving it a smooth finish.

STEP ELEVEN: FINISH THE TABLE

With any varnish, there will usually be a chemical odor, so avoid bringing the table into your home until it airs and is completely dry.

Apply the varnish according to the instructions from the manufacturer. Using a shop rag, rub the varnish in, working with the grain of the wood. Again, take your time with this step, as this

is where you get to bring all your hard work and planning to life. I typically use Good Stuff urethane gel for a more natural but refined and protected finish on my furniture. That's just my preference.

STEP TWELVE: ENJOY!

Let your varnish job cure for a few days. Once it is dry, you are ready to bring your new slab table inside and use it! Watch for wear and tear. If you notice the wood drying out, you can add another coat of varnish. Another option, for an even quicker fix, is to use wood conditioner, which can add life back to your table without the headache of resurfacing and aid in the longevity of the slab.

Enjoy!

> PRO TIP: *For benches to accompany the table, buy the same stock and repeat these steps but with different dimensions. Typical bench height is 18 inches with a seat depth of 15 inches.*

SAFETY TIPS

Ask a friend for help when lifting heavy lumber and plywood.
Make sure you are comfortable using a track saw, drill, and sander.
Always wear the proper safety glasses.
If you have long hair, tie it back.
Keep fingers away from the saw blade and drill bit.

The making does not end here. The creative possibilities are endless.

My dream for you as you read this book is that you learn how to tap into your creativity, to open up your creative third eye, and to light and nurture the spark that pushes you forward—free of judgment. I hope that these pages have inspired you to create things that move you and that you will find confidence even in mishaps and begin to see life in a state of creative flow.

Each of the DIY projects in this book is meant to contribute to a larger goal: hosting a dinner party! As I've mentioned, my community has always been there to catch me when I fall, to help me brainstorm new ideas when I'm stuck, and to lend a hand when I need it. The DIY projects in this book—table, benches, daybed, cutting boards, coasters, and wood-dyed napkins—will give you everything you need to host *your* community. Invite the members of your life who support you, encourage you, and love you. Break bread together at your table, eat off your cutting boards, and host your friends and family on the beautiful pieces you have created though this book.

It has been an honor to guide you through this process. Thank you for sharing this journey. As creatives, we are all in it together and we are more than capable of doing anything that we want.

WITH GRATITUDE . . .

This book has been a journey for me. As a first-time writer, I found that a lot came up. This new creative process was just as much about me learning and growing as it was about imparting what I've experienced. More than anything, it has been a deep dive inward. I have challenged my foundations and strengthened what those ideas were built on. This book would have never been possible were it not for my father, who raised me to speak my mind, forge my own path, never let gender define me, and humbly work my ass off toward anything I want to achieve, no matter how hard the times were. These pages are dedicated to him. I love you, Papa.

To my family, my two sweet sisters, Alana and Faith Marie, these pages are also for you, as an extension of the two of you. You have been there through it all, the highs, the lows, and the in-betweens.

Alana, you are my soul, and we are traveling this world as kindred spirits, my best friend and my world. Faith Marie, the world is yours: Take it, breathe it in, and live present in every moment. I love you. Thank you for always reminding me of our roots, of the power we hold, and the love you never cease to share. Your support means the world to me.

To my love, Antrom, you have been there pushing me along, reminding me of my strength, being my mirror, my guiding light, my biggest fan. These words would not have seen the light of day if not for your guidance and unconditional love and support and for pushing me to be my highest self. Thank you for being my partner, my right hand in the shop, my building partner, and my favorite human being. Thank you for shooting so many (most) of the photos in this book, for helping me build and create the DIY projects, and for being there through it all.

This book is what it is thanks to the incredible group of badass females whom I get to surround myself with, work with, and be constantly inspired by. Thank you, Katie Gong, my best friend and soul mate, for teaching me your woodshop ways, for guiding me, inspiring me, problem-solving with me, loving me, and being the greatest wifey and best friend a girl could ever ask for. Thank you for shooting photos of the book with me and for long days in the shop building with me, helping me create content and working with me on these DIY projects. I respect all that you are. This book truly would not be possible without you. To Meryl Pataky, thank you for always being honest with me, truly pushing me to be the best artist and human I can be, for taking me seriously, for opening my eyes to new ways of creating, and for welcoming me into your craft that I am endlessly inspired by. You always show up for and support me and remind me of my power. To Joanna Riedl, this book would not have been possible without you. You have been more than an editor: You are my family, my sister, my mentor, my therapist, and my dear friend. This process has brought us together so tightly and I value your light immensely. I am constantly humbled by your grace and wisdom. Thank you for being my mirror and reminding me of who I am always. To Jen Woo, who is another reason these pages feel like my soul pouring out onto paper. Also so much more than my editor, you are my dear friend who from the moment I met you saw the light in me and shared yours so intimately, bringing me in, challenging my beliefs, and pushing me forward. Your words are like butter, and your passion inspires me to create with meaning. To Nathalia Vieira, you keep my ass in line, you guide my soul, you hold my heart, and you truly keep me so organized. Your tenderness and outspoken heart remind me to be the same. Thank you for guiding me in this wild life and for being family. To Gabriela Adams, you are my rock, my dear friend who has seen me for who I am and who I can be. Your light brightens my path and your strength has inspired and guided me through so much. Thank you, Kathrin and Brian Smirke, for opening up your home for me to come and photograph my projects in. You two are the kindest, most giving humans I know. Thank you, Veronica, from Rock Bound Oasis Retreat, for opening up your inspiring land to me and allowing me to shoot photographs for this book. Marissa Lace, thank you for your endless encouragement. You have never ceased to show up for me, hype me, and show me love. Thank you for your big, beautiful heart. Thank you all for the roles you have played in my life and for being the reason this book exists. I love you with all my heart.

Thank you to the incredible contributors of these pages: to Megan Mussari of Apprvl for showing us the ways of textiles;

Kristen Morabito for your stunning illustrations; Tanya Jones for guiding me and these pages through a beautiful meditation; David Roost of Roostmade for creating a custom wood butter just for this book; Antrom Kury for helping me design and build so many of these DIY projects; and Katie Gong for your beautiful DIY creations and building.

Thank you, Sequoia Diner, for creating a stunning meal for the culmination of the book. Your vision inspires me and I am truly humbled that you wanted to work with me. So thankful for our beautiful Oakland community. Sophie James Wine, thank you endlessly for being a part of the last photo shoot of the book and contributing your delicious wine! You are a powerhouse and I am so deeply inspired by how hard you work and the brand you have created. Thank you to the Wild Fig for a stunning artisan charcuterie board and for being a part of the dinner and culmination of the book. Katie Gong, your wood knots are the showstoppers; thank you always for helping me out!

REFERENCES

LUMBER/MATERIALS

HOME DEPOT
www.homedepot.com

LOWE'S
www.lowes.com

MACBEATH HARDWOOD
www.macbeath.com

HARBOR FREIGHT
www.harborfreight.com

HOME DECOR

CB2
www.cb2.com

KATIE GONG
www.katiegongdesign.com
IG @katie.gong

LOSTINE
www.lostine.com
IG @lostineathome

KÜDD:KRIG HOME
www.kuddkrighome.com
IG @kuddkrighome

FOUR / QUARTER
www.fourqtr.com
IG @four_quarter

SAFFRON + POE
www.saffronandpoe.com
IG @saffronandpoe

WORLD MARKET
www.worldmarket.com

SHEPHERDESS
www.shepherdess.co
IG @shepherdesshides

SOUKIE MODERN
www.soukiemodern.com
IG @soukiemodern

MARISSA LACE
www.lightloveandlace.myshopify.com
IG @marissalace

PARACHUTE HOME
www.parachutehome.com
IG @parachutehome

WEST ELM
www.westelm.com

FLORA GRUBB GARDENS
www.floragrubb.com
IG @floragrubbgardens

APPRVL
www.apprvlnyc.com
IG @apprvl

GENERAL STORE
www.shop-generalstore.com
IG @generalstore

SHOP ON THE MESA
www.shoponthemesa.com
IG @shop_onthe_mesa

MIDLAND SHOP
www.shop-midland.com
IG @midland_shop

KOSA ARTS
www.kosaarts.com
IG @kosa_arts

WONDER VALLEY
www.welcometowondervalley.com
IG @wondervalley

ROOSTMADE
www.roostmade.co
IG @roostmade

URBAN OUTFITTERS
www.urbanoutfitters.com
IG @urbanoutfitters

RESTORATION HARDWARE
www.restorationhardware.com

JUNGMAVEN
jungmaven.com
IG @jungmaven

PENDLETON
www.pendleton-usa.com
IG @pendletonwm

ART

KATIE GONG
www.katiegongdesign.com
IG @katie.gong

MERYL PATAKY
www.merylpataky.com
IG @merylpataky.com

MINERAL WORKSHOP
www.mineralworkshop.com
IG @mineralworkshop

SAM LEE
www.samleehello.com
IG @samleehello

SVEN CERAMICS
www.svenceramics.com
IG @svenceramics

LUVHAUS
www.luvhaus.com
IG @luvhaus

KATHRIN SMIRKE
www.bandsofcolor.com
IG @kathrinesmirke

WEST PERRO
www.westperro.com
IG @westperro

HEATHER DAY
www.heatherday.com
IG @heatherday

TANYA JONES
www.takecarebeautymagic.com
IG @take_care_beauty

LIFESTYLE

THE JOSHUA TREE HOUSE
www.thejoshuatreehouse.com
IG @thejoshuatreehouse

THE SHACK ATTACK
www.weareinourelement.com
IG @the_shack_attack

VENTANA BIG SUR
www.ventanabigsur.com
IG @ventanabigsur

ROCKBOUND OASIS RETREAT
IG @rockboundoasisretreat

THE ASSEMBLY
www.theassembly.com
IG @theassemblysf

BRIGHT SIDE COLLECTIVE
www.bright-side.co
IG @brightsidecollective

WEST COAST CRAFT
www.westcoastcraft.com
IG @westcoastcraft

UNDER CANVAS
www.undercanvas.com
IG @undercanvasofficial

AMANGIRI
www.aman.com/resorts/amangiri
IG @amangiri

EL REY COURT
www.elreycourt.com
IG @elreycourt

OJO CALIENTE MINERAL SPRINGS
www.ojocaliente.ojospa.com
IG @ojospa

SEQUOIA DINER
www.sequoiadiner.com
IG @sequoia_diner

SOPHIE JAMES WINE
www.sophiejameswine.com
IG @sophiejameswine

THE WILD FIG
IG @thewildfigco

ABOUT THE AUTHOR

Aleksandra Zee is an artist, woodworker, designer, teacher, traveler, explorer, and public speaker. With a degree in fine art, Zee builds large- and small-scale wooden wall hangings, installations, and furniture, creating original and commissioned pieces out of her woodshop in Oakland, California. From taking trips to the high desert to spending time in front of the ocean to frolicking among the trees, Zee draws her inspiration from travel, nature, and personal experience. She lives in Oakland with her partner, Antrom Kury, and their dog, Jack.

DEY ST.

HarperCollins books may be purchased for educational, business, or
sales promotional use. For information, please email the Special Markets
Department at SPsales@harpercollins.com.

FIRST EDITION

Designed by Renata De Oliveira
Photography by Antrom Kury, featuring photographs by Katie Gong
Editor: Joanna Riedl
Second Editor: Jen Woo

Library of Congress Cataloging-in-Publication Data has been applied for.

ISBN 978-0-06-287862-5

19 20 21 22 23   LSC   10 9 8 7 6 5 4 3 2 1